STEVEN CARL McCASL

Steven Carl McCasland is th   Director of
the Beautiful Soup Theater C   University
graduate, Steven's critically acc   d plays have been seen in
New York and Bermuda. In 2009, Steven was commissioned to
adapt poet Jack Wiler's anthologies into a solo performance
about Wiler's struggle with HIV. That play, *Fun Being Me*, was
workshopped with Jack in the title role before his passing in
2009. Steven's other plays include *When I'm 64*, *Hope & Glory*,
Opheliacs Anonymous, *Blue*, *Pulchritudinous* (First Place,
Huntington Award in Playwriting), and *Billy Learns About
Captain Kirk* have all received productions regionally and in
Manhattan. In June 2011, Steven premiered his original
adaptation of Lewis Carroll's *Alice's Adventures in Wonderland*.
Setting Wonderland in the heart of Paris, he also directed and
was featured in the cast as the Mock Turtle. After its one-week
workshop, *Alice Au Pays Des Merveilles* was picked up for an
extended run at the SoHo Playhouse through September. His
acclaimed play *neat & tidy* made a splash on the Bowery in
May of 2012, with critics hailing McCasland as a new Thornton
Wilder and the play as one of the top dramatic plays of the year.
After critically acclaimed workshops of Steven's plays and
What Was Lost in 2014, Beautiful Soup partnered with the
Clarion Theatre to present five of his plays in repertory in 2015.
Also featured in rep were *28 Marchant Avenue*, *Der
Kanarienvogel* (*The Canary*) and a revival of *neat & tidy*. His
writing has been acclaimed by New York critics as 'brilliant',
'riveting', 'mesmerising' and 'extraordinary'.

Steven Carl McCasland

LITTLE WARS

NICK HERN BOOKS

London

www.nickhernbooks.co.uk

A Nick Hern Book

Little Wars first published in Great Britain in 2021 as a paperback original by Nick Hern Books Limited, The Glasshouse, 49a Goldhawk Road, London W12 8QP

Little Wars copyright © 2021 Steven Carl McCasland

Steven Carl McCasland has asserted his moral right to be identified as the author of this work

Cover image: Rebecca Pitt

Designed and typeset by Nick Hern Books, London
Printed in the UK by Mimeo Ltd, Huntingdon, Cambridgeshire PE29 6XX

A CIP catalogue record for this book is available from the British Library

ISBN 978 1 83904 003 0

Woodland
CARBON
www.woodlandcarbon.co.uk
NICK HERN BOOKS
Printed on Carbon Captured paper

Little Wars received its world premiere at The Clarion Theatre, New York City, in 2015, with the following cast:

GERTRUDE STEIN	Polly McKie
ALICE B. TOKLAS	PennyLynn White
LILLIAN HELLMAN	Kimberly Faye Greenberg
DOROTHY PARKER	Dorothy Weems
AGATHA CHRISTIE	Kimberly Rogers
MARY (MURIEL GARDINER)	Kristen Gehling
BERNADETTE	Samantha Hoefer
Director	Steven Carl McCarsland
Producer	The Beautiful Soup Theater Collective

The play received its international premiere at the Daylesford Theatre, Hamilton, Bermuda, in 2016, with the following cast:

GERTRUDE STEIN	Susanne Notman
ALICE B. TOKLAS	Heather Conyers
LILLIAN HELLMAN	Gillian Henderson
DOROTHY PARKER	Deborah Pharoah-Williams
AGATHA CHRISTIE	Karen Stroeder
MARY (MURIEL GARDINER)	Emily Ross
BERNADETTE	Raven Baksh
Director	Carol Birch
Producer	Jennifer Osmond for The Bermuda Musical and Dramatic Society

The play received its US regional premiere at Mixed Blood Theatre, Minneapolis, Minnesota, in 2017, with the following cast:

GERTRUDE STEIN	Candace Barrett Birk
ALICE B. TOKLAS	Sue Scott
LILLIAN HELLMAN	Vanessa Gamble
DOROTHY PARKER	Elizabeth Desotelle
AGATHA CHRISTIE	Alison Edwards
MARY	Laura Adams
(MURIEL GARDINER)	
BERNADETTE	Miriam Schwartz
Director	Shelli Place
Producer	Elena Gianetti for PRIME Productions

The play received its digital premiere and was streamed internationally in November 2020, with the following cast:

GERTRUDE STEIN	Linda Bassett
ALICE B. TOKLAS	Catherine Russell
LILLIAN HELLMAN	Juliet Stevenson
DOROTHY PARKER	Debbie Chazen
AGATHA CHRISTIE	Sophie Thompson
MARY	Sarah Solemani
(MURIEL GARDINER)	
BERNADETTE	Natasha Karp
Director	Hannah Chissick
Digital Creative Editor	John Walsh Brannoch
Producers	Thomas Hopkins & Michael Quinn for Ginger Quiff Media in association with Guy Chapman & Bailey Harris Kelly

Acknowledgements

This play went through a number of drafts. The feedback of friends and colleagues was invaluable, and they all must be thanked: Thia Stephan Hyde, Jon Imparato, JoAnn Mariano, Patti Mariano, Polly McKie, Carey Purcell, Molly Tiede, Maggie Wirth, Shelli Place, Debbie Chazen, Catherine Russell, Juliet Stevenson, Ginger Quiff Media and all of the other actresses, directors and designers who have worked on this play. Especially Carol Birch, who helped me discover things I never knew were there.

Great thanks to Georganne Guyan Bender, Charles Busch, Robert Featherstone, Irma and Sol Gurman, Julie Halston, James Horan, Lucille Kenney, Rich Kizer, Alison Broomfield and Logan Rollins for their unwavering support and encouragement.

Overwhelming gratitude to Albert J. Pica, Theresa Pica and Susan Percoco.

Thanks are due to Nora Ephron, whose *Imaginary Friends* introduced me to Lillian Hellman and Mary McCarthy when I was sixteen. She helped inspire this and every play that followed.

And, of course, to Lillian Hellman.

*This play is dedicated to Irma Gurman and Elaine Tozar,
two teachers who inspired a life of learning*

Characters

GERTRUDE STEIN, *sixty-five. The hostess. A Lesbian writer with no interest in the conventional. American*
ALICE B. TOKLAS, *sixty-two. Gertrude Stein's lover, secretary and muse. Art enthusiast and collector. American*
LILLIAN HELLMAN, *thirty-four. A lying, chain-smoking, conniving woman who also happens to be a brilliant writer. American*
DOROTHY PARKER, *forty-seven. Satirist and author. Despite her biting wit, Dorothy cowers to Lillian out of respect and fear. American*
AGATHA CHRISTIE, *forty-nine. A crime-fiction writer. Far too smart for her own good. British*
MARY (MURIEL GARDINER), *thirty-eight. A psychiatrist working in the Austrian underground to rescue Jews and dissidents. American*
BERNADETTE, *twenty-two. Gertrude and Alice's maidservant. German*

Time and Place

22 June 1940. Gertrude Stein and Alice B. Toklas's country home in the French Alps.

Gertrude Stein and Alice B. Toklas' country home in the French Alps. 22 June 1940. France will fall to Germany in less than twenty-four hours. A piano sits in one corner of the stage, paintings and easels in every other. Some canvases are complete, some are barely touched. A sofa and coffee table down left, an armchair not far away. There are candles burning in some places; a lamp glowing on a tabletop next to the armchair. A half-drunk glass of Scotch sits on the table, too. But more than anything, there are books. Fiction, poetry, plays, essays, biographies, notebooks, sketchbooks. More than you can imagine. At curtain, BERNADETTE, *a maidservant of twenty-two, cleans nearby. After a moment, she speaks to us in a hushed and urgent whisper.*

BERNADETTE. 'I'll tell you when I'm dead,' I said. She tilted her head. Stupefied. That's what Gertie would've called her. 'I'll tell you when I'm dead and buried.' 'But if it's a story worth telling – ', she said, ' – then tell it!'

GERTRUDE (*off*). There is a ghost in this book.

BERNADETTE. 'Yes,' I told the student. 'But for every story worth telling, there's a dozen secrets worth keeping.'

GERTRUDE (*entering*). I repeat: there is a ghost in this book.

ALICE (*off*). There is no ghost in the book.

GERTRUDE. I open it and I hear Him.

ALICE *enters with a drink and stands in the stage-left doorway. She is a petite woman, plainly dressed, and diminutive in every way to* GERTRUDE.

ALICE. It's a Him?

GERTRUDE. Oh, yes.

ALICE. If there *were* a ghost in your book, how would you know it's a Him?

GERTRUDE. He has a very deep voice.

ALICE. Perhaps it's Marlene Dietrich.

GERTRUDE. Don't be absurd. It's Yeats.

ALICE. Of William Butler?

GERTRUDE. Yes.

ALICE. Because that isn't absurd?

GERTRUDE. There is a ghost in this book, Alice, in this book, there is a ghost and when I open it, I can hear Him.

ALICE. Yeats?

GERTRUDE. Listen.

They listen for a moment. Silence. Beat.

ALICE. Agatha will be here any minute.

GERTRUDE. Who?

ALICE. Agatha! You invited her.

GERTRUDE. I?

ALICE. Yes. You'd read her essay –

GERTRUDE. I, Gertrude?

ALICE. Of Stein, yes. And you wrote her.

GERTRUDE. I don't remember.

ALICE. You invited her, Gertrude. And she'll be here any minute.

GERTRUDE. 'An intellectual hatred is the worst.'

ALICE. Do not quote Yeats, please.

GERTRUDE. He is speaking through me and I am speaking through Him.

ALICE. You're drunk on Scotch.

GERTRUDE. '*Wine comes in at the mouth*
And love comes in at the eye;

That's all we shall know for truth
Before we grow old and die.'

ALICE. You must stop grieving, Gertrude.

GERTRUDE. One cannot grieve words.

ALICE. Then you must stop sulking.

GERTRUDE. I am not sulking, I'm reading!

ALICE. Agatha will be here very soon. And she is bringing *guests*.

GERTRUDE. Guests?

ALICE. Yes, so, please put away the Yeats and the Scotch and the grief.

GERTRUDE. Grief and reflection are two very different things. What guests is Lady Conan Doyle bringing?

ALICE. Don't call her that.

GERTRUDE. How about Aggie?

ALICE. Just stick to Agatha.

GERTRUDE. I shall not 'stick' to anything. When have you known me to 'stick', Alice?

ALICE. Not now, Gert.

GERTRUDE. I, Gertrude Stein, invited Agatha Christie to dinner, and by dinner I mean alcohol, and Agatha Christie has decided to return the favour by bringing guests?

ALICE. Two Americans.

GERTRUDE (*with sudden interest*). She is bringing Americans?

ALICE. Yes.

GERTRUDE. There are Americans in Europe besides us?

ALICE. I asked the same!

GERTRUDE. Who?

ALICE. It's a surprise.

GERTRUDE. Tell me who, Alice!

ALICE. Oh, I'd better not…

Beat.

GERTRUDE. Not Lily.

ALICE. Oh, dear.

GERTRUDE. Not Lily Ann Fucking Hellman.

ALICE. It's just for a few hours! We'll have a few drinks and –

GERTRUDE. Lily Ann is a contemptible bore.

ALICE. She and Yeats have that in common.

GERTRUDE. *Must* you speak ill of the dead?

ALICE. Oh, really, Gertrude! You hated William when he was alive.

GERTRUDE. And now that he's dead, I can appreciate him.

ALICE. Then just picture Lillian dead, too.

GERTRUDE. I've tried that. It doesn't work.

ALICE. Then try harder. They'll be here any minute.

GERTRUDE. Who is the third?

ALICE. Dorothy Parker.

GERTRUDE. Who?

ALICE. A writer.

GERTRUDE. *Everyone* is a writer.

ALICE. You will like her.

GERTRUDE. Or perhaps I will hate her and she will hate me or perhaps she will like me and I will like her and *why* are they coming?

ALICE. You invited them!

GERTRUDE. I most certainly did not invite Lily Ann Hellman.

ALICE. She hates it when you separate the syllables like that.

GERTRUDE (*proudly*). I know.

ALICE. Please don't pick a fight tonight, Gert –

GERTRUDE. Lily Ann is the fighter and I am the debater. There is a difference. This is a salon and in salons we debate about fighting instead of fighting about debating.

ALICE. But Lillian –

GERTRUDE. – is a bitch.

The doorbell rings.

ALICE. That's them.

BERNADETTE *enters from offstage and makes her way to the door.*

GERTRUDE. Thank you, Bernadette.

BERNADETTE. Of course.

GERTRUDE. That is a lovely dress, Bernadette.

ALICE. Don't flirt.

GERTRUDE. Gertrude Stein does not flirt.

ALICE. She flirted with me.

GERTRUDE. I merely wrote a poem.

ALICE. Has Miss Stein written *you* any poems, Bernadette?

BERNADETTE. Not lately, Miss Toklas.

GERTRUDE. Do I detect jealousy?

ALICE. You detect boredom. I'd like another poem.

GERTRUDE. Then another poem you shall have.

'*I love my love with a v*
Because it is like that
I love my love with a b
Because I am beside that
A king.'

ALICE. And I think Bernadette wants one too...

> *She presses her forehead against* GERTRUDE*'s as* BERNADETTE *opens the door.*

BERNADETTE. Hello.

MARY. Hello, I – I'm looking for a Miss Toklas.

GERTRUDE. Miss Toklas is preoccupied with poetry.

ALICE. Nonsense. Don't listen to her. She is a bored old woman.

MARY. I'm very early, I'm afraid –

GERTRUDE. I am not old for I am young.

ALICE. Let her in, Bernadette!

> BERNADETTE *lets the woman in. She is an American in her thirties. Beautiful and petite. The women stare at each other for a moment.*

MARY. Mary? (*Beat.*) I'm Mary –

> *Beat.*

ALICE. Oh, dear, we weren't expecting you until tomorrow!

MARY. There's been a development. I must take an earlier train. You must be Miss Stein...

GERTRUDE. Of the Gertrudes, yes.

ALICE. Would you like to sit? A drink? Surely you must be *thirsty*!

GERTRUDE. Scotch works well on Alpine evenings.

MARY. I shouldn't.

ALICE. Then, perhaps your coat –

MARY. Excuse me. (*To* BERNADETTE.) Would you please...? (*To* ALICE.) I think perhaps we should be alone, Miss Toklas.

ALICE. Yes, of course. Bernadette, could you –

GERTRUDE. What? Could she what? Could she leave?

MARY. Yes.

ALICE. We should have privacy.

GERTRUDE. There is no privacy in a house of writers.

MARY. I'm sorry if I've offended you –

GERTRUDE. I am not easily offended. Unless of course you are Lily Ann Hellman. Then – *then* the very sight of you would offend me. You haven't offended me, Mary. You've merely made an error.

ALICE. Gert.

GERTRUDE. Bernadette has served me coffee. And tea. And Scotch. And wine. She's brought me paper and ink. And she has made my bed and fluffed my pillows. Once, she held me while I cried because I was blocked and couldn't write and when a writer cannot write she dies ten thousand deaths. And if she can serve me coffee and tea and Scotch and wine and bring me paper and ink and make my bed and fluff my pillows and hold me while I die ten thousand deaths and do all that while knowing there is Jew in my blood, she can stay for this conversation.

Beat.

MARY. I'm sure Ethel has told you, but –

GERTRUDE. Yes –

MARY. – each mission requires one hundred and fifty francs. Fifty for the passport, fifty for the guard to look the other way, and another fifty for the boat. It may seem steep, but –

ALICE. We understand.

GERTRUDE. And how will you get the passports across the border?

ALICE. And the money, too –

MARY. It will be sewn into the lining of my hat.

ALICE. Who will we be helping?

MARY. There are many who are waiting.

ALICE. Children?

MARY. Yes.

GERTRUDE. Women?

MARY. Yes.

   Beat.

GERTRUDE. Three. We can help three –

ALICE. Make sure one is a child.

GERTRUDE. And one is a woman.

MARY. And the third?

ALICE. Kind.

GERTRUDE. Smart.

ALICE *and* GERTRUDE. Both.

MARY. I promise you it will only be used for good.

   Beat.

GERTRUDE. Wait here.

   GERTRUDE *exits.*

ALICE. Will you be safe?

MARY. Yes.

ALICE. And where will you stay until the train leaves?

MARY. I will wait at the station for Ethel. She'll arrive after
   sunrise. The train departs at nine-thirty –

ALICE. You'll stay there all night?

MARY. Yes.

ALICE. But won't that seem suspicious?

MARY. I'll just miss the last train. I'll be stranded. Forced to stay. No one will bother the helpless American.

ALICE. Why not stay here? Leave when you must, but at least stay the night.

MARY. Thank you, but I can't.

ALICE. You need to rest! You can't possibly sleep in the station.

MARY. I've done it before.

ALICE. How?

MARY. With one eye open.

ALICE. But an American in Europe during wartime, Miss...

MARY. Last names aren't important.

ALICE. Surely, they must be suspicious of you.

MARY. Americans are safer.

ALICE. For now, perhaps.

MARY. There are always questions, Miss Toklas. But this isn't my debut. There's been at least a hundred missions already.

ALICE. Incredible!

MARY. Oh, it's certainly gotten a bit more dangerous since I first began. I've been back in America for quite some time, though. When we left, my husband and I, we had to board our daughter with a governess. In Vienna. We couldn't take her with us.

ALICE. How ever did you stand it?

MARY. Without sleeping. I returned to bring her home with me a few days ago, but they asked me to assist on a, uh... Well, they needed someone a bit more – skilled for this particular mission.

ALICE. They needed an American.

MARY. That too.

ALICE. You really should stay the night. The house is warm. And we've plenty of food. (*Beat*.) And company, too!

MARY. Company?

ALICE. Soon, yes. We're having dinner guests –

MARY. I must be going, then!

ALICE. Why?

MARY. The more people who know, the more dangerous it becomes, Miss Toklas.

GERTRUDE *re-enters with an envelope*.

ALICE. No one will know your secret but us.

MARY. It is very difficult keeping secrets from friends.

GERTRUDE. They're not our friends.

ALICE. Gertrude and I have been keeping secrets for many years. From friends and from foes.

GERTRUDE. We have mastered the Art of Lying. Four hundred and fifty francs. Three passports. Three Jews.

MARY. Thank you, Miss Stein. Miss Toklas, thank you –

GERTRUDE. If I am to respect myself, Miss…

MARY. Mary.

GERTRUDE. What is your last name?

MARY. Last names aren't important.

ALICE. Our friends will want to know.

GERTRUDE. They are not our friends. They're writers –

MARY. Writers!

ALICE. American writers, too…

MARY. In Europe!

GERTRUDE. Not all. There's an Anglo…

MARY. Are they very good?

GERTRUDE. That's questionable.

MARY. Writers… (*Beat.*) Perhaps…

GERTRUDE. What? Perhaps what?

MARY. Perhaps I will stay…

GERTRUDE. Then you will most certainly need a surname.

Beat. She gives in.

MARY. Buttinger.

GERTRUDE. Very well. Fetch Mary Buttinger some Scotch, please, Bernadette! (*To* MARY.) It will warm your innards.

MARY. No, I really shouldn't –

BERNADETTE *exits.*

ALICE. Please. Your coat.

MARY. I must keep my wits.

ALICE. And are those wits inside your coat pockets?

Beat. MARY *allows her to take the coat.* ALICE *goes to hang it.*

GERTRUDE. Sit with me on this sofa, Mary Buttinger.

They sit.

Where did this begin?

MARY. What?

GERTRUDE. Your story. Your mission.

MARY. Oh. Necessity.

GERTRUDE. You are providing a remarkable service, Mary Buttinger.

MARY. As are you.

GERTRUDE. Nonsense.

MARY. These funds will go a long way.

GERTRUDE. If I am to maintain any sense of self-respect, Mary Buttinger, I must do what is right for my people. That I am safe and others are not is –

MARY. You're surviving!

GERTRUDE. I am cowering. It has not been easy. It has not been easy being an American Jew living in France. I have cheated myself and my people to survive.

MARY. But look at what you've just given me. Look at what you've done!

GERTRUDE. There are some people who think I'm a hypocrite. And perhaps I am. To keep us safe. Alice and I. (*Beat.*) Everybody knows if you are too careful you are so occupied in being careful that you are sure to stumble over something and I do not wish to stumble over my conscience, Miss Buttinger. I do what I can in silence, and say what I must out loud.

MARY. But someone must tell the story. Forgive me, Miss Stein, but if we remain silent, no one will ever know! Politicians should be politicising. Preachers should be preaching. Writers should be writing… Silence will only mean death.

BERNADETTE *re-enters with a drink. She brings it to* MARY, *who does not drink.*

GERTRUDE (*after a beat*). The drink wishes to be drunk.

MARY. Aren't you going to have one?

GERTRUDE. I've had several.

ALICE. A fact.

GERTRUDE. And so has Alice.

ALICE. Another fact.

MARY. Oh…

GERTRUDE. Go on. The drink wishes to be drunk.

MARY *brings the drink to her lips, but is stopped before sipping.*

Wait!

ALICE. Oh, dear.

GERTRUDE. She hasn't any ice!

ALICE. Bernadette, she hasn't any ice.

BERNADETTE. Oh. But Miss Stein never takes any in –

GERTRUDE. But I am sure Mary Buttinger does.

Beat.

MARY. I do.

GERTRUDE. I am a rare kind of bird.

ALICE. And we're two birds of a feather.

GERTRUDE. I will get you the ice. Bernadette, I will get the ice.

BERNADETTE. No, no –

GERTRUDE. Nonsense. Sit. Your feet deserve a rest, so rest your deserving feet.

BERNADETTE. But –

GERTRUDE. When the doorbell rings, you may assume the position. Lily Ann will expect it.

BERNADETTE *reluctantly sits in the armchair, as...*

ALICE. Fuck!

GERTRUDE. What?

ALICE. I'm sorry, Miss Buttinger, I do not use that word very often, but *fuck*!

GERTRUDE. What is it?

ALICE. I still haven't changed! I was going to change my clothes!

GERTRUDE. Why?

ALICE The way Lillian will look at me.

GERTRUDE. Lily Ann can piss up a rope. Ice! (*Exits*.)

ALICE. Excuse me, Miss Buttinger. Bernadette will keep you company.

MARY. But –

ALICE. I'll only be a moment. (*Exits*.)

Beat.

MARY. Who is Lily Ann?

BERNADETTE. Lillian Hellman.

MARY. Lillian Hellman as in… Lillian Hellman?

BERNADETTE. Yes.

MARY. The playwright?

BERNADETTE. Yes.

MARY. Well.

BERNADETTE. Yes.

MARY. Does this happen very often?

BERNADETTE. Yes.

MARY. It must be very exciting. All those writers –

BERNADETTE. Maybe for some.

MARY. What brought you to this house?

BERNADETTE. I worked in a café. And I served them wine.

MARY. Who?

BERNADETTE. Miss Stein and Miss Toklas.

MARY. You served them wine.

BERNADETTE. Yes.

MARY. And now you're their housekeeper.

BERNADETTE. More than that.

MARY. You're not telling me everything.

BERNADETTE. The wine was everything.

MARY. It must have been very good wine.

BERNADETTE. They have been kind to me. When I needed kindness most, they were kind to me. Isn't that enough of a reason?

MARY. But it's a little odd, don't you think? The sheepish little country girl comes to work for the radical lesbians? There's a story there.

BERNADETTE. Perhaps you are a writer too, Miss Buttinger...

MARY. You can call me Mary.

GERTRUDE *re-enters, deep in thought, holding a tong and an ice cube.*

GERTRUDE. Have you ever thought about how ice can only melt because it is already frozen and the opposite of freezing is melting but perhaps it is also thawing and if the ice can only melt that is a sad existence because always melting must be lonely –

MARY. Miss Stein, I think I will stay the night, after all.

GERTRUDE. Well, then! Melt away. (*Drops the ice cube into the glass.*)

MARY. If you really don't mind –

GERTRUDE. Of course not! But I'm afraid that means, my dear Bernadette, that you must be on your way and make up a bed for Mary Buttinger.

MARY. Oh, I –

BERNADETTE. Of course.

BERNADETTE *exits, passing behind them.*

MARY. Bernadette is very young.

GERTRUDE. She needed to be rescued. There are no other motives, Mary Buttinger.

MARY. I wasn't insinuating that –

GERTRUDE. We are lesbians, Mary Buttinger. Not animals.

MARY. Of course.

GERTRUDE. Some people forget things. I do. We move on.

MARY. Yes.

GERTRUDE. Tell me. Why have you gone into this line of work, Mary Buttinger? Tell me.

MARY. It was the right thing to do.

GERTRUDE. Who told you that?

MARY. Myself, I think.

GERTRUDE. You either know or you don't know. You can't be simple and think at the same time. Who told you it was the Right Thing to Do?

MARY. I did.

GERTRUDE. You.

MARY. Yes.

GERTRUDE. Of the Buttingers.

MARY. Yes.

GERTRUDE. You were correct. I am not as brave.

MARY. But you are! You're helping. That's brave.

GERTRUDE. I must do what I can if I am to look myself in the eye. (*Beat.*) The Jews have produced only three originative geniuses: Christ, Spinoza, and myself. And how can a genius turn its back on an entire race?

MARY. What did you mean when you said you were 'rescuing' her? Bernadette.

GERTRUDE. There are joys in being a lesbian, Mary Buttinger. Joys beyond the physical. And the joys are joyous because you do not come into contact, well, not often, with the other race. (*Beat.*) With Men. (*Beat.*) Have you ever been penetrated deep and rough with no sense of pleasure? Gored like a matador in a crowded arena as the bull rips out your innards like spaghetti?

MARY. No.

GERTRUDE. Bernadette has.

ALICE *re-enters cheerfully.*

ALICE. This will have to suffice for Lillian.

GERTRUDE *blows a raspberry.*

MARY. Excuse me for asking, but exactly who is Lillian?

GERTRUDE. A bitch.

ALICE. A writer.

MARY. Then Bernadette wasn't joking.

GERTRUDE. Bernadette never jokes. Not even about Lily Ann Hellman.

The bell rings.

ALICE. That will be them.

MARY. But the hat –

ALICE. Quickly, then. We'll hide it in the closet…

ALICE *and* MARY *put the money into the seams of the fur hat and bring it to the closet.*

GERTRUDE. Funny, that: three Jews hiding in a fur hat in the French Alps in a closet in a house where cowards live.

ALICE. We aren't cowards, Gert.

BERNADETTE *enters, making her way to the door.*

GERTRUDE. But we are safe and they are not.

MARY. You can't save them all.

Beat.

GERTRUDE. They are not flowers in a windstorm, Mary Buttinger.

MARY. Aren't they, though?

The hat is hidden and the door is being opened. LILLIAN *enters first, pulling off her gloves and shrugging off her coat.* BERNADETTE *catches it before it falls.* LILLIAN *is followed by* DOROTHY. LILLIAN *is clearly unamused by her surroundings.*

LILLIAN. Some digs, Gert.

GERTRUDE. Lily Ann.

DOROTHY. You must be Miss Toklas.

LILLIAN. Careful, Dottie. That's the maid.

ALICE. She's kidding. And you can call me Alice, Miss Parker.

DOROTHY. Must I?

ALICE. Please. Your coat? And Lillian, your hat?

LILLIAN. Maybe later. I'm glad you didn't pick up on account of us.

GERTRUDE. Pick up what?

LILLIAN. This and that.

DOROTHY. Ignore her, Miss Stein. She's only teasing. Hello. (*Extending a hand to shake.*) Dorothy Parker.

GERTRUDE. Hello.

They shake hands. Sort of.

You're a writer?

DOROTHY. Yes. Just like you.

GERTRUDE. I doubt that.

LILLIAN. Ignore her, Dorothy. She's only boasting. Gertrude loves to boast.

GERTRUDE. Of course, I love to boast. Everyone loves to boast. Don't you?

DOROTHY. I certainly do.

LILLIAN. And who are you?

MARY. Mary. (*Beat*.) Buttinger.

ALICE. Where is Agatha?

LILLIAN. Mary Buttinger? What have you written?

ALICE. Did Agatha come with you?

GERTRUDE. She isn't a writer, Lily Ann.

DOROTHY. She took a separate car.

LILLIAN. What, then? A sculptor?

MARY. A psychiatrist.

> *Long beat*. LILLIAN *is not enthused*.

ALICE (*cheerfully changing the subject*). Was Agatha far behind?

DOROTHY. Only a few miles, I think. She doesn't like the way Lillian drives.

> LILLIAN *sits on the couch*.

LILLIAN. It's paranoia.

DOROTHY. Lillian likes to speed.

LILLIAN. Agatha likes to crawl.

GERTRUDE. I would've thought it was the reverse!

LILLIAN. Despite your modest surroundings, Gertrude, do tell me. Where are you hiding the Scotch?

ALICE. Bernadette will get that for you.

GERTRUDE. No ice! (*Sits in the armchair.*)

LILLIAN *pats the couch, inviting* MARY *to join her.* DOROTHY *sits on the other side, sandwiching* MARY *between them.*

LILLIAN. And what exactly is an American psychiatrist doing in the French Alps in the middle of a war?

MARY. I am visiting family.

LILLIAN. Good to have family in Europe during a war. Don't you think?

GERTRUDE. Dorothy. Dot. Dottie.

DOROTHY. Dorothy will do.

GERTRUDE. I like Dot.

DOROTHY. It doesn't really matter what you like. My name is Dorothy.

Beat.

GERTRUDE. I'm afraid I've never heard of you. What do you write, Dot?

DOROTHY. Everything.

GERTRUDE. Be specific.

DOROTHY. Poetry. Stories, too.

LILLIAN. And criticism.

DOROTHY. That's the easy bit.

GERTRUDE. What sort of criticism?

DOROTHY. Whatever sort I feel like. Theatre. Cinema. Books. *Tuesdays*. You know –

GERTRUDE. Criticism seems such a waste of words. What do you write well, Dot?

DOROTHY. Everything.

LILLIAN. I do believe Gert has finally met her match.

GERTRUDE. In what?

LILLIAN. Arrogance.

DOROTHY. I prefer to call it 'confidence'.

GERTRUDE. Did you come to pick a fight, Lily Ann?

LILLIAN. I'm only having a little fun!

GERTRUDE. Fun!

LILLIAN. Only a little fun, Gert. Now, tell me. Has your maid
     gone to Scotland for the Scotch? (*An evil giggle.*) Is she
     distilling it herself?

GERTRUDE. I do not engage with terrorists.

DOROTHY. Lillian speaks very highly of you, Gertrude

GERTRUDE. Does she?

DOROTHY. Yes.

GERTRUDE. I do not care for liars or lying.

LILLIAN. I've said it before, Gert. You're very talented.
     Ferocious, but –

GERTRUDE. Ferocious? I?

ALICE. Gertie, please.

GERTRUDE. I, ferocious?

LILLIAN. Yes, but some of your work is quite moving –

GERTRUDE. Some?

LILLIAN. Yes.

DOROTHY. She can't possibly like all of your –

GERTRUDE. Can't she? Is it physically impossible to
     appreciate an author's entire canon?

DOROTHY. Name one. Name an author whose every word you
     hang on.

GERTRUDE. Ernest Hemingway.

LILLIAN *blows a raspberry.*

ALICE. Oh, dear.

GERTRUDE. What? What, Lillian?

LILLIAN. The man is a hack.

GERTRUDE. Don't you dare –

LILLIAN. Every single word just reeks of booze. Can't you smell it when you open the pages? And all that *anger.* (*Beat. To* MARY.) Have you ever had a glass thrown at you by Ernest Hemingway?

MARY. No –

GERTRUDE. If she had, she would've deserved it.

BERNADETTE *enters with the glass of Scotch for* LILLIAN.

LILLIAN (*reaching for the drink*). Finally!

GERTRUDE. No!

GERTRUDE *knocks it from* BERNADETTE*'s hand and into* LILLIAN*'s lap.*

LILLIAN. Christ, Gert!

GERTRUDE. Lily Ann Hellman will not drink my Scotch tonight.

LILLIAN. My dress!

GERTRUDE. Your dress, your dress, who cares about your dress?

LILLIAN. I care about my dress, thank you very much! Christ!

ALICE. Why did you have to do that, Gertrude?

GERTRUDE. Stay out of it!

ALICE. Bernadette, please get Miss Hellman another drink.

LILLIAN. And a towel!

GERTRUDE. No!

BERNADETTE *heads for the kitchen.*

LILLIAN. Oh, this will stain! Christ, Gert!

GERTRUDE. Buy another! No Scotch for the bitch, Bernadette.

BERNADETTE *stops.*

ALICE. Gertrude, please!

GERTRUDE. Please what?

ALICE. Don't!

GERTRUDE. Don't what?

ALICE. This is no time for games. Bernadette, a towel, please.

BERNADETTE *begins to exit.*

GERTRUDE. Absolutely not. Let it air-dry!

BERNADETTE *stops again.*

ALICE. Please, Bernadette. Miss Stein is having a tantrum.

GERTRUDE. She isn't drinking my Scotch!

LILLIAN. Christ! I don't want the goddam Scotch. Just a fucking towel, *s'il vous plaît.* (*Beat.*) Now, Bernadette? Please!

BERNADETTE *scurries off.*

GERTRUDE. Don't yell at my maid like that! And stop saying 'Christ'. You're a Jew! You're not fooling anyone.

LILLIAN. Oh, Gertie, shut up. You're drunk.

Beat.

GERTRUDE. That is a fact.

LILLIAN. And you're being very nasty to dear Alice.

GERTRUDE. There is no such thing as being good to your wife.

LILLIAN. She is a very patient woman.

GERTRUDE *blows a raspberry at* LILLIAN.

DOROTHY. Perhaps we should go.

GERTRUDE. Nonsense.

DOROTHY. But –

ALICE. This is what they do, Miss Parker.

DOROTHY. It's like being back at The Algonquin.

ALICE. I imagine. It's something about the two of them together... like oil and water.

GERTRUDE. Like salt on a slug!

ALICE. But they haven't killed each other.

GERTRUDE *and* LILLIAN. Yet.

ALICE. See? An agreement! They come along rarely, Miss Parker, but they do happen.

Beat.

GERTRUDE. Fine. (*Rises.*) A Scotch. Do you want ice?

LILLIAN. No.

GERTRUDE. Well, that's too damn bad, because you're getting the fucking ice, Lily Ann.

GERTRUDE *exits.*

ALICE. Did you want something too, Miss Parker?

DOROTHY A gin and tonic, please.

ALICE. A staple of mine. I like your taste. (*Exits.*)

DOROTHY. Is she flirting with me?

LILLIAN. Don't be an idiot.

DOROTHY. I don't know many lesbians. Then again, there *is* Edna Ferber. (*Beat.*) Gertrude is…

LILLIAN. Yes. (*Pointing at* MARY *and changing the subject.*) You. Miss Buttinger, or is it Doctor –

MARY. Mary. Please.

LILLIAN. I never liked 'Miss Hellman' much either. Then again, Lillian isn't anything special. Oh, it would've been fine if it were just a flower. But then they had to go and add the 'Ann' and butcher a perfectly lovely name like Lily. Arthur used to call me that. Lily. Even on our wedding day he said, 'I, Arthur Kober, take Lily Florence Hellman to be…' And somewhere in the room I heard my mother scoff. Of course, it didn't last. He was a theatrical agent, would you believe? Always smelling like cheap cigars and counting every single penny. Don't get me wrong, darling. For every ounce of sex appeal he lacked, Arthur was kind. One can't have the complete Don Juan without always suspecting something. And when I divorced the bore in 1932, I remember my friend Dottie, she said, 'You could've had him for breakfast.' (*Beat.*) She was right. I could've. But at least he called me Lily. Now, Dash… Oh, Dashiell likes Lillian. He says it's strong. 'And a man like Dashiell Hammett deserves a strong woman.' And when Dash says it, when he says Lillian, it's like he's making love. So, even with the vulgar 'Ann' attached, the flower's grown on me. (*Beat.*) Have you got a fella, Mary?

MARY. Yes. (*Beat.*) He's a doctor also. A psychologist.

LILLIAN. And have you heard of *me*?

MARY. Of course. I saw *The Children's Hour*, my husband and I –

LILLIAN. And what did you think?

The bell rings.

DOROTHY. That will be Agatha. (*Rises.*)

LILLIAN. Sit down.

DOROTHY. But –

LILLIAN. The help will get it, Dorothy. What did you think of my play, Miss Buttinger?

MARY. It's a very good play.

> BERNADETTE *enters and opens the door to reveal* AGATHA CHRISTIE. *She is dressed elegantly, but conservatively. Her hair is perfectly coiffed.*

DOROTHY. The Great Agatha Christie! (*Rising to greet her.*) How was your trip?

AGATHA. Fine. Where is the hostess? Hello, Lillian.

LILLIAN. Agatha.

AGATHA. Don't get up.

LILLIAN. I won't.

AGATHA. Haven't changed a bit, I see. Where is the hostess?

DOROTHY. Making drinks.

AGATHA. Perfect. (*To* BERNADETTE.) You. What is your name?

BERNADETTE. Bernadette.

AGATHA. A vodka gimlet, please. Quickly.

BERNADETTE. Yes.

AGATHA. No olives.

BERNADETTE. Yes.

AGATHA. I detest olives. (*To* MARY.) Who are you?

LILLIAN. This is Mary Buttinger.

AGATHA. I've never heard of her. (*To* MARY.) Are you a writer? What have you written?

MARY. I'm not a writer.

LILLIAN. She's a psychiatrist. Can you believe it, Agatha?

AGATHA. Positively dreadful! A psychiatrist? And an American, too? What exactly do you do, my dear? Give them Altoids when they're sad?

MARY. It's a great deal more than that –

AGATHA. And just what is an American psychiatrist doing in France in the middle of a war?

MARY. I suppose I could ask the same of a British mystery writer.

AGATHA. That's an easy case, darling. Don't you think? I've been invited to a dinner party. I sincerely doubt you flew all the way from – where, exactly? By your accent, I'd assume somewhere in the north-eastern part of America. New York, perhaps?

MARY. New Jersey.

AGATHA. Did you fly here? Or did you take *Queen Elizabeth*?

MARY. The *Queen Elizabeth*.

AGATHA. I see.

MARY. I'm visiting my cousin.

GERTRUDE *enters, followed by* ALICE. GERTRUDE *gives* DOROTHY *her gin and tonic, and begins to drink a Scotch.*

LILLIAN. Is that mine?

GERTRUDE. Eventually.

After one last sip, she passes LILLIAN *the glass. As they greet* AGATHA, LILLIAN *wipes the rim of the glass with a handkerchief.*

ALICE. Ah! Our honoured guest!

AGATHA. I? Honoured?

ALICE. The Great Agatha Christie!

AGATHA. Why does everyone keep calling me that?

GERTRUDE. Would you prefer 'decent'?

AGATHA. I've just been getting to know your cousin, Gertrude.

GERTRUDE. My cousin?

AGATHA. Yes. Mary. I never knew you had a psychiatrist for a cousin!

MARY. I'm not – We aren't cousins.

LILLIAN. If they were, I'd imagine Mary would've helped Gertrude with her marbles a long time ago.

AGATHA. Then how do you two know each other? Forgive my curiosity but –

DOROTHY. Forgiven!

AGATHA. – I never imagined Gertie keeping company with a shrink.

GERTRUDE. She attended one of my lectures and we began a correspondence. Now, stop fishing. If you want to fish, go for a swim!

ALICE. Tell me, Lillian. Have you written anything new?

GERTRUDE. Oh, yes! Another play about a bunch of lonely schoolgirls? All that pent-up sexual frustration?

LILLIAN. The new play is much different.

GERTRUDE. Thank goodness. Are you finally writing something about which you actually understand?

LILLIAN. Oh, I understood every bit –

GERTRUDE. Did you?

ALICE. Don't, Gert –

GERTRUDE. Did you understand how awful you made us look? Not just women, but lesbians –

DOROTHY. Don't be absurd.

GERTRUDE. You enjoyed that, Dottie?

DOROTHY. Dorothy. And yes. I enjoyed that play very much. And so did a *slew* of other people.

LILLIAN. Miss Buttinger did!

GERTRUDE. A bunch of grown women behaving like children! Cruel and taunting and evil. And then there was, oh, there was the rumour. The Creation.

LILLIAN. It was a plot device, Gert. Nothing more, nothing less.

GERTRUDE. It made us look so ugly.

LILLIAN. That wasn't my goal, Gertie. I was trying to show desperation –

GERTRUDE. What does Lillian Hellman know about desperation? What do you know about us? About what it's like being us? Being abnormal? Being abnormal vampires?

LILLIAN. No one ever said anything about vampires –

GERTRUDE. You made us look like a bunch of fools! Like savages!

DOROTHY. Lesbians, you mean?

GERTRUDE. And women!

Beat.

ALICE. It was a wonderful play, Lillian. But it wasn't easy for us to see.

LILLIAN. Gertrude –

DOROTHY. Read her the review.

ALICE. What review?

DOROTHY. Lillian's new play.

GERTRUDE. Does she carry it around in her purse?

LILLIAN. Gertrude, it was theatre. I never meant to say –

DOROTHY. Read them the new review, Lily.

LILLIAN. It was escapism!

DOROTHY. It's much different.

GERTRUDE. Have we got any earplugs?

ALICE. Lillian is a wonderful writer.

DOROTHY. It's very good. Tallulah's in it.

GERTRUDE. Tallulah Shmallulah!

ALICE. I think I might've read about it. In the paper. *The Little Horses*, or something like that.

DOROTHY. Foxes, darling. *The Little Foxes*.

GERTRUDE. How many lesbians are there?

DOROTHY. You should see it, Gertrude. Lily's play.

GERTRUDE. That would require going back to America, wouldn't it?

LILLIAN. And what's so wrong with that?

GERTRUDE (*taking* ALICE's *hand*). A million things, Lily Ann. A million things.

DOROTHY. I saw it again just before we left. I'd promised Tallullah that I would. And I always keep my promises. After the performance, she wanted to go out for a drink.

LILLIAN. Tallulah *always* wants to get a drink.

DOROTHY. But she was in one of her moods and no matter where we went, the light was too bright, the light was too dim, the band was too loud, the pianist didn't know her song. Before we'd even had a single drop of gin, we'd walked all the way to 92nd Street, all the way up until every single corner was alive with jazz.

 MARY. Harlem, then?

DOROTHY. Mecca, darling.

LILLIAN. I'll never understand it. Dorothy Parker and her ni–

DOROTHY. Don't.

LILLIAN. What?

DOROTHY. You know what you were going to say.

LILLIAN. What? Friends. I was only going to say –

DOROTHY. Just don't, Lillian.

   Beat.

ALICE (*changing the mood*). I imagine it's quite something. Harlem, I mean.

DOROTHY. It's poetry in motion, Alice, darling. Everyone and everything tastes like bathtub gin. And even better is once they realise you're one of them, that you belong, even better, Alice, darling, is when someone invites you to dance!

LILLIAN. Absurd.

DOROTHY. I'd just sat through your play for the fourth time, Lillian. Forgive me for making a little room for fun.

ALICE. It sounds magical.

GERTRUDE. Parisian.

DOROTHY. Oh, yes, Gertrude. Parisian indeed.

GERTRUDE. Paris is the Centre of the Universe.

LILLIAN. Maybe yours.

ALICE. Ours, Lillian.

LILLIAN. It certainly isn't any more. It'll be gone soon.

GERTRUDE. You're wrong there. What? Will they box up the Eiffel Tower? Cut it into a thousand tiny pieces and box it up? It will simply go away? On a holiday!

LILLIAN. With the way things are going, Pétain will be handing it over to Hitler any moment.

AGATHA. Please, let's not –

GERTRUDE. Give me your drink.

LILLIAN. What?

GERTRUDE. Give me your drink, Lily Ann. You will not drink my liquor!

LILLIAN. You're insane.

GERTRUDE. Regardless of that fact, give me your drink.

ALICE. Gertie, calm down.

GERTRUDE. You heard her.

ALICE. Yes, but –

GERTRUDE. You heard her and you want me to calm down.

ALICE. Your ulcer –

GERTRUDE. This is our home. Do you understand that, Lily Ann? France is our home. It is our roof and our floor and our walls and our carpet and our windows. It's a house.

LILLIAN. And even houses fall. I don't say it to be cruel. I just prefer realism over fantasy.

GERTRUDE. Is that a fact?

Beat.

LILLIAN. Most of the time. Yes.

AGATHA. Couldn't we please change the subject? Maybe to something just a little less depressing?

GERTRUDE. You know, Pétain may have his faults, Lily Ann, but he certainly cares about our country.

LILLIAN. But this isn't your country, Gertrude. You're an American. Just like me. Alice too.

GERTRUDE. Not any more.

ALICE. We're happier here, Lillian.

MARY. What will come of the Jews if Hitler marches in?

GERTRUDE. I can only hope that will not happen.

MARY. But if it does?

GERTRUDE. Pétain will do what he needs to so France will survive.

LILLIAN. Mmmm. At what cost? And whose?

DOROTHY. I need another drink.

LILLIAN. Don't we all, darling?

ALICE *stands behind* GERTRUDE's *armchair,* DOROTHY *joining* LILLIAN *on the couch.* AGATHA *is bored and desperate to change the conversation.*

AGATHA. You are a painter, too, Gertrude?

GERTRUDE. I am an artist of art.

AGATHA. I see. (*She doesn't.*)

DOROTHY. May I... (*Her glass is empty.*) Another drink, please?

ALICE (*calling off*). Bernadette! I'm a collector, Miss Christie.

AGATHA. You have some very... interesting pieces.

GERTRUDE. Interesting is what interests us. (*Beat.*) Or it did.

ALICE. The luxuries of art seem a trifle selfish these days.

BERNADETTE *re-enters.*

ALICE. Please get Miss Parker another drink, Bernadette.

BERNADETTE *takes* DOROTHY's *glass. During the conversation,* MARY *meanders to the window. She stares out of it, hovering nervously.*

AGATHA. The 'luxuries' of art?

GERTRUDE. Yes, they are luxurious.

AGATHA (*laughing*). I'm sorry, Gertrude, but the life of an artist is anything but luxurious.

GERTRUDE. How many bedrooms do you have?

AGATHA. What's *that* got to do with anything?

GERTRUDE. The Great Agatha Christie does not live
luxuriously?

AGATHA. Don't be absurd. Of course I do. But I'm a mystery
writer, Gertrude. Not an artist. Artists are... bohemian.

GERTRUDE. We're bohemian, Alice, dear.

ALICE. All right...

BERNADETTE *re-enters with another drink for*
DOROTHY.

GERTRUDE. I've forgotten. What's a bohemian?

AGATHA. The Queen of Wordplay can't remember what a
bohemian is?

GERTRUDE. I've begun forgetting things. And besides, I want
to hear your definition.

AGATHA. They're vagabonds. Of a sort.

GERTRUDE. And what is a vagabond?

AGATHA. Gertrude, please –

GERTRUDE. Please *you*, I've begun forgetting things. Go on.
What is a vagabond?

AGATHA. A gypsy.

GERTRUDE. A gypsy?

AGATHA. This is foolish.

GERTRUDE. Says the fool.

DOROTHY. Perhaps if we took the dictionary off the shelf –
Have you got a dictionary, Miss Toklas?

ALICE. Somewhere, yes... (*Begins searching.*)

DOROTHY. Maybe there's several definitions.

AGATHA *joins* MARY *at the window.*

GERTRUDE. There are three legitimate and one supposed writer in the room this evening, Dottie, nobody needs a dictionary.

DOROTHY. Well, you're the one who forgot what it meant in the first place.

AGATHA. See anything interesting out there, dear?

MARY. Cold.

AGATHA. You can't see cold.

MARY. But you can imagine what it looks like.

AGATHA. I'm on a mountain with a madwoman.

GERTRUDE. Oh, we're all mad here, Aggie.

LILLIAN. Perhaps you *are* Gertrude's cousin after all, Miss Buttinger. Without the forgetting, I hope.

GERTRUDE. I couldn't find my keys two mornings ago.

DOROTHY. They're always the first things you lose.

GERTRUDE. And then I lost six words.

LILLIAN. It comes with age.

GERTRUDE. What do you know of age?

LILLIAN. I've heard things.

GERTRUDE. I have begun the process of forgetting and there are things I'd like to remember and thoughts I'd like to think. I write them down.

DOROTHY. Like what?

GERTRUDE. The first time I tasted Alice's lips. They tasted like venison.

ALICE. I'd just eaten –

GERTRUDE. Also the word 'pulchritudinous'. My keys because I need them. The sound of a Klezmer fiddle on a cobblestone street. How to scream. I love to scream. The way Alice combs her hair so perfectly all while counting one, two, three, four, eight-six, eighty-seven, ninety-nine, one hundred. How to write a haiku.

LILLIAN. A haiku for you:

> *'Look at old Gertrude.*
> *She's forgotten her mind and*
> *Left it on the stove.'*

GERTRUDE. One cannot forget one's mind.

DOROTHY. Isn't that the last thing to go?

GERTRUDE. I'll die before that day comes. My stomach will eat me from the inside out.

AGATHA. Perhaps you should eat something, then.

MARY *suddenly turns to the group.*

MARY. Are you a friend of the Jews, Miss Christie?

AGATHA. What sort of a question is that?

MARY. A valid one these days. And as the only one in this house who is not a Semite or even just a little bit Semitic –

AGATHA. You're awfully bold!

MARY. Are you a friend of the Jews, miss?

AGATHA. Jews can read, can't they?

MARY. Is that a yes?

GERTRUDE. I believe it is as close to a yes as you will get, Mary.

MARY. How do you feel about Adolf Hitler?

DOROTHY. Oh, dear.

AGATHA. The man is a ninny!

DOROTHY. I think I need another drink.

AGATHA. And that moustache!

ALICE. It certainly is a silly-looking moustache.

DOROTHY (*chuckling*). Do you think Eva enjoys it?

ALICE. Oh, I don't know…

DOROTHY. Do you think it tickles her fancy?

GERTRUDE. I question his taste.

MARY. Is that all?

GERTRUDE. Oh, I question many things.

AGATHA. Tell us.

GERTRUDE. I question the moon and insist it is a lamp. I question a dog and declare it is a cat. I question the sky and ask why it is blue. Did it steal the ocean's suit and run away with the spoon? Who I question and proclaim, 'You are a fork!' I question Hitler's moustache and pronounce he is Charlie Chaplin. What is the answer?

Beat. No one responds.

Nothing? (*Beat.*) No answer? (*Beat.*) Not even a guess? (*Beat.*) Then, what is the question?

MARY. What happens next?

LILLIAN. We wait.

MARY. Or we fight.

LILLIAN. Fight who? Hitler?

MARY. Yes!

LILLIAN. America isn't going to get involved.

MARY. And you're satisfied with that?

LILLIAN. It isn't my problem.

MARY. But you're a Jew!

LILLIAN. I am also a woman. And a writer. And a lover. (*Her glass is empty.*) And thirsty. (*Rising.*) Would you like another drink too, Mary?

DOROTHY. I would!

BERNADETTE *collects their glasses and exits.*

MARY. It's that easy for you?

LILLIAN. What, dear?

MARY. Looking away.

LILLIAN. I have looked away many times before.

MARY. There are people dying. Women and children.

LILLIAN. But not by my hand.

MARY. Is that the legacy you want to leave behind?

GERTRUDE. Perhaps no one ever gets a complete history of anyone. When my bones are dust, who will remember me? When my eyes have been eaten by worms and maggots and time, what will become of my memories? Will they wilt? Dry up? And if they do, who will I be? Who will *you* be? A blip. A minuscule moment. A bunch of pages in a book collecting dust.

MARY. And that's if the book survives!

GERTRUDE. What happens when they come for those? What happens when they toss us in the furnace and strike the match? Say goodbye to your characters. Because if no one remembers them, Lillian, who will remember you?

LILLIAN. Everyone dies, Gertrude. It's a part of life!

MARY. Not like this, it's not.

AGATHA. Careful, Miss Buttinger. If one sticks too rigidly to one's principles, one would hardly see anybody.

MARY. But that's exactly what we need right now, Miss Christie. Principles! We can *all* do more. Including Marshal Pétain, I'm sorry to say, Miss Stein, Miss Toklas.

ALICE. You aren't wrong, my dear.

AGATHA. But can you *prove* it? Can anyone actually prove the rumours?

MARY. Of the camps? Why would *anyone* doubt them?

AGATHA. Because rumours, Miss Buttinger, can spread like wildfire. And they never end where they started. And because these are...

LILLIAN. Horrific.

AGATHA. Yes. Forgive me, but I appreciate evidence. And I wonder if it's just as bad as all you rabble-rousers say.

MARY. Everyone keeps saying that. Everyone keeps saying, 'Oh, it's not so bad, the camps don't exist...' But if they don't exist and if it's not so bad, then where is everyone disappearing to? (*Beat.*) The truth isn't a ball of clay. You can't twist it and manoeuvre it and shape it and change it. It's a brick. It's a two-tonne anchor.

LILLIAN. Says who?

GERTRUDE. The universe.

LILLIAN. Isn't that what we do, though? Don't we twist the things that happen to us and sell them between two hard covers?

AGATHA. I certainly don't.

LILLIAN. There isn't just a little bit of Agatha Christie in those pages? Not even a subconscious memory tucked away somewhere? None of your characters ever go *missing*? Disappear for *weeks*?

Beat. She doesn't answer.

See? It's human for a writer. We all do it!

GERTRUDE. Speak for yourself! My truths are truths and my fictions are fiction. There are no in-betweens.

MARY. It will only get worse. It might not be 'so bad' now, but it will get worse. (*Rises.*) I think I should be going.

GERTRUDE. No! Do not let Lily Ann Hellman run you out of this house! (*Turning to* LILLIAN.) You're a hack. Do you know that, Lily? You are a –

LILLIAN. And what are you? (*Rises.*) You string a bunch of words together –

GERTRUDE. I pour out my heart! You spew out your bile.

LILLIAN. I need to use the powder room. (*Starts to exit.*)

ALICE. Oh, it's down to the left –

GERTRUDE. You're going to run away?

LILLIAN. I'm not running away, Gertrude, I'm going to powder my nose.

GERTRUDE. For who? For me? You're not my type!

GERTRUDE *stalks her off stage and we hear a door slam.*

ALICE. Gertrude! (*To the others.*) Excuse me. (*Exiting.*) Gertrude, just give her a moment!

GERTRUDE (*off*). Don't pay any attention to her!

ALICE (*off*). You're being absurd!

AGATHA. Oh, dear…

GERTRUDE (*off*). She'll come out eventually!

DOROTHY. That would be a good thing for them to cut on my tombstone…

ALICE (*off*). You know, she's sensitive!

GERTRUDE (*off*). Sensitive? Lily Ann Hellman is about as sensitive as a *porcupine*!

We hear a door slam.

MARY. Do you think they'll come back?

AGATHA. Of course.

MARY. Even Miss Hellman?

AGATHA. Once you stop paying attention to her, she always comes back for more. (*Beat.*) What exactly is a psychiatrist doing *here*?

MARY. Oh. I...

BERNADETTE. Miss Stein and Miss Buttinger have been pen pals for quite some time.

MARY. Yes... I thought it would be nice to pay her a visit.

AGATHA. And what about your husband? Where is he?

MARY. In America. He has a practice of his own.

AGATHA. Does he? Psychiatry?

MARY. Psychology.

AGATHA. I'm afraid I never understood the difference.

MARY. Psychiatry is for the treatment of mental disorders and psychology is the study of them. (*Beat.*) In a nutshell.

AGATHA. I wasn't actually asking. But thank you. I'll try to remember that the next time I meet a psychiatrist. And what about you, Bernadette? Do you have a husband?

BERNADETTE. No.

AGATHA. No children then?

BERNADETTE. No.

AGATHA. They are blessings in disguise. Rosalind certainly was. My daughter. She's nineteen now.

BERNADETTE. I was nineteen once.

AGATHA. Would you like them? Children, I mean?

BERNADETTE. I –

AGATHA. Not everyone does. Maybe when you find yourself a husband. Rosalind is, of course, from my first husband. Archibald. Dreadful man. A scoundrel, really. But I loved him. And I kept his name, would you believe it? But then again, how does one let a name like Agatha Christie get away? It would be suicide for a writer. Even if Archie *was* a philandering bum from Chudleigh.

MARY. Is that why you disappeared? I read about it, you know –

AGATHA. Even in America?

MARY. It was world news, Miss Christie.

AGATHA. World news! Because a woman needed a little peace and quiet –

MARY. They thought you'd been kidnapped! Or worse –

DOROTHY. Murdered.

AGATHA. Nonsense. I got in the car and I drove. After I'd found out about her, about Archie's little friend, about Nancy Neele, I got into the car and I drove. That's all! I kept on driving until I couldn't keep my eyes open, wandered into a little hotel in a town too small to remember and asked for a room. I didn't think he'd recognised me, even as I signed the registrar as 'Neele' instead of Christie. But once the papers declared me dead or missing or kidnapped, my face was all over Britain. And the nosey little man behind the desk suddenly realised who this Miss Neele really was.

MARY. Didn't you think to call anyone? To tell them where you were?

AGATHA. Who? My maidservant?

MARY. Anyone!

AGATHA. I was surprised they'd even noticed I'd left, Miss Buttinger.

MARY. Don't you think it's a little unfair?

AGATHA. When your husband leaves you, you'll understand.

MARY. I hope I never do.

AGATHA. I suppose it was a good thing, though. That the man from the hotel recognised my face. If he hadn't, I might *never* have come home. And I might never have met Max.

And Max is a wonderful man. My second husband, you
see… An archaeologist. I thought that would be exciting but
the dirt and the dust, you know, it's hell on your hands and
the stains never come out of your trousers. But there's a
benefit to it all, I suppose. The older I get, the more he
appreciates me! If you marry a man, my dear, marry an
archaeologist.

BERNADETTE. Maybe… Some day.

AGATHA. He is, though. Wonderful, I mean. Sometimes I have
to remind myself. I thought I'd have another child with Max,
but it just hasn't happened. (*Beat.*) Sometimes I think he
loves the pyramids more than me!

Laughter.

DOROTHY. I believe we need more refreshments.

AGATHA. Haven't you had enough?

DOROTHY. I am surrounded by giants. Let me drink.

AGATHA. How many?

DOROTHY. I lost count.

AGATHA. Moderation is good for the soul.

DOROTHY. And so is gin. Bernadette, please. (*Beat.*) I do not
like my state of mind. I'm bitter, querulous, unkind. But
when I drink, the days are easier. Shorter instead of longer.
But sometimes it takes a little more than one or two to make
me tight. And tonight is one of those nights.

AGATHA. What does Alan think of your drinking?

DOROTHY. Alan? Ha! The man is queer as a billy goat. I found
him last week in bed, you know, with a boy. Younger, too.
Maybe sixteen. A tiny little thing with hips smaller than mine.
But I knew. You see, I knew these things going in. I knew these
things when I said 'Yes'. But Alan is – There is a friendship
there. We spar. He meets my sullenness with bitterness and
sees my rage and raises me his grief. What does Alan think of
my drinking? We share glasses. He tastes my lipstick when he

finishes off my gin. He sucks on ice I've left behind. What does Alan think of my drinking? He drinks of my drinking. What did your Archie think? When you ran away?

AGATHA. That isn't fair.

DOROTHY. But it's what you did. Isn't it? I stay. I might drink, but I stay. I face the demons and I slay the dragons and I drink to quench my thirst after battle.

AGATHA. And what about the scars on your wrist?

Beat.

DOROTHY. I got these in battle with a dragon. He was thirty feet tall but didn't breathe fire. Just ice. Endless ice. And not the kind that clinks in your glass, but the kind that keeps you up at night, that freezes your toes off, the kind that makes your chest feel like it might explode. But halfway through this battle, I learned the dragon had a name. Charles the Dragon. Charles MacArthur the Dragon.

AGATHA. The playwright.

DOROTHY. The dragon! And we talked, this dragon and I, about life and love and liquor and language and the thing I forgot was that when you're drinking, talking can lead to accidents. And I'm sure that's all we did. Talked. But there it was, plain as day. Or there it wasn't. And Charles the Dragon gave me thirty dollars, do you believe it? He put thirty dollars in the palm of my hand and he told me to get rid of it. To put it in a box and put it on the top shelf and never look at it again. And I did. I had a gin and tonic while I waited for the cab and another when the driver started honking. And then I took the thirty dollars and I went to the doctor's and I did as the dragon said and I got rid of it. (*Beat.*) I need another drink.

AGATHA. When did you – ?

DOROTHY. Ten years ago. He would've been ten. Or she. Ten years old. I keep thinking that some day I might stop punishing myself, but –

BERNADETTE. You can't forget a memory like that.

Beat.

DOROTHY. No... No, Bernadette. You can't. I want one though. A baby, I mean. Some day. (*Beat.*) Another drink? Please?

AGATHA. A weak one.

DOROTHY (*to* MARY). And you?

MARY. Nothing. Thank you.

DOROTHY. No. A baby. (*Beat.*) Have you got one?

MARY. A daughter. Yes.

DOROTHY. A treasure.

An awkward silence. ALICE *enters.*

ALICE. I apologise if you heard us –

AGATHA. Nonsense. People argue.

ALICE. Gertrude argues. I speak.

AGATHA. Don't you get tired?

ALICE. Doesn't everyone?

AGATHA. It must be exhausting.

ALICE. It is. But the good kind.

DOROTHY. There is no such thing as the Good Kind.

ALICE. Then the satisfying kind. Besides. My hair has not greyed that much.

AGATHA. How ever did you find each other?

ALICE. Paris.

AGATHA. There's more to it than that.

ALICE. People come into our lives, Miss Christie. What more is there to say?

DOROTHY. They might come, but they don't always stay.

AGATHA. I thrive on details. Forgive me, Alice, darling, but I do. I crave them.

ALICE. We both needed saving, Gertie and I.

AGATHA. Go on.

ALICE. I went to the market and came back with a needle and thread to sew up the hole in my heart. I was a little thing then, and the pieces of me broke easily. Youth can be a deadly thing for a hopeless romantic. And so I fled. It was a September morning in 1907 when I stepped off the boat and onto Parisian soil. There was so much to see. But my eyes went straight to a collection of very blue, very sad paintings. You could almost hear them breathing. A bearded man was selling them. Gertrude's brother, Leo. And Gertie was sitting nearby, buried in a book… She's always buried in a book. And even though I should've been on bed-rest because my heart was still sewn up with stitches, my feet were moving faster than the rest and I bought a painting I couldn't afford just so that I could learn her name. (*Beat.*) We went for a drink that evening. At a little café right on the edge of the Seine. It was the first time I ever noticed how rosy Gertrude's cheeks get when she drinks too much. And it was the first time I ever noticed the lines in her forehead that crinkle when she laughs. And it was the first time I ever danced with someone to silence. (*Beat.*) It was always like that, then. With Gertrude, every single day was an adventure. And I do so like adventures. (*Beat.*) Leo detested me. Or maybe he detested the love Gertrude had for me. And one day when it was raining, I knocked on the door and Leo refused to let me in. I was turning into a puddle right before his eyes, and he closed the door in my face. And I remember, he told me I was abnormal. (*Leo really said this to* ALICE. *Don't brush it off…*) That we were abnormal and I was an abnormal vampire. He returned to America the next morning, and I hung my clothes in his closet.

DOROTHY. You love her.

ALICE. With every fibre of my being. (*Beat.*) It isn't easy, but it's true. This. Us. It isn't always good, but it's real. It isn't always there, but it's here. I don't mind the sullenness. Or the mood-swings. Or the stories. Or the exaggerations. Or the hours. Or the days. Or the years. (*Beat.*) Gertrude is Gertrude and Alice is Alice and the days are long and the nights are longer but her body is angry and she gets these ulcers and she thinks her stomach will eat her alive and the doctor says it might so I take the sullenness and the mood-swings and the stories and the exaggerations and the hours and the days and the years because without the years there won't be any memories and I want to remember the way she turned needle and thread to glue. Time is always moving even when we beg Him to stand still. (*Beat.*) She'll die first and leave me here.

AGATHA. You can't know that.

ALICE. I know Gertrude. And Gertrude will die first. And then I'll spend the next twenty years waiting until I see her again.

GERTRUDE (*entering*). Lillian has barricaded herself in the bathroom and refuses to come out.

AGATHA. Oh, for Heaven's sake. Haven't you got a key?

GERTRUDE. I swallowed it.

AGATHA. You didn't.

GERTRUDE. You're right. I didn't.

AGATHA. Just unlock the door, then.

GERTRUDE. Why? Do you actually enjoy talking to Lily Ann?

AGATHA. I wouldn't leave you in a bathroom all evening, Gert.

GERTRUDE. If only you were as kind to your victims. (*Sits.*)

ALICE. We'll just give her a little space and she'll be out in no time.

MARY. Perhaps I should leave.

GERTRUDE. Nonsense.

MARY. I never meant to cause –

GERTRUDE. How about another drink, Bernadette? For all of us. Sit down, Mary.

BERNADETTE. Of course. (*Taking* AGATHA*'s glass*.) A gimlet with no olives for Miss Christie. She detests olives. (*Exits*.)

AGATHA. Where did you find such a bright girl, Gert? I might have to steal her away.

GERTRUDE. We listed an advertisement in the paper.

MARY. An advertisement?

GERTRUDE. I do love an echo.

MARY. But Bernadette said –

GERTRUDE. Bernadette never says.

MARY. But just a little while ago she –

GERTRUDE. Just a little while ago she what?

MARY. She said she served you wine. At a café.

GERTRUDE. Oh.

ALICE. Oh, yes.

GERTRUDE. That is true.

ALICE. She applied for the ad after she served us wine.

    BERNADETTE *re-enters with drinks*.

GERTRUDE. We recognised her.

MARY. I see…

ALICE. A happy accident.

GERTRUDE. Happy slappy.

AGATHA. And I'm the Queen of Sheba. Spill the beans. Where'd you find her?

BERNADETTE. Does it really matter? (*Beat.*) I'm sorry, Miss Christie. I do not mean to be rude, but does it really matter where they found me?

AGATHA. I was going to ask how much they paid you and offer you double, but now –

BERNADETTE. I wouldn't take it. They have been good to me. This is my home. I could never leave them.

ALICE. We enjoy Bernadette's company. She is –

GERTRUDE. A member of our family.

MARY. And you are – I'm sorry, Bernadette, but you're... German?

BERNADETTE. Yes.

GERTRUDE. We met in Berlin.

MARY. And it doesn't bother you that –

BERNADETTE. What?

MARY. That they're – I'm sorry – That Miss Stein and Miss Toklas are...

BERNADETTE. I am German *Jewish*, Miss Buttinger.

MARY. Oh, I apologise. I didn't –

AGATHA. You have a German Jew in your house?

GERTRUDE. Yes.

AGATHA. But the risk!

GERTRUDE. Isn't that part of life? Taking risks? Surely the great Agatha Christie must know about taking risks.

AGATHA. Not with Adolf Hitler breathing down my neck, I don't.

ALICE. We couldn't leave her there. In Berlin? How could we leave her behind?

GERTRUDE. If it weren't for our passports, I don't think we'd have even been there in the first place. But I was there to read some poetry.

ALICE. Of course, they probably burned all the copies a few months later.

DOROTHY. Awfully brave of you.

GERTRUDE. What would be the point of waking up tomorrow if I had no one to read to?

AGATHA. Pretty soon there won't be anyone to read to here, either. Can't you hear their boots? I hear them every day. Getting closer and closer.

GERTRUDE. Pétain will not let our country fall.

AGATHA. And what if he does? Oh, sure, *you've* got American passports. But what about her? What about Bernadette?

GERTRUDE. That won't happen here. Not in France.

DOROTHY. Don't be so sure, Miss Stein. Even perfection fades.

ALICE. I think perhaps we should change the subject.

AGATHA. Why?

GERTRUDE. Alice is right.

AGATHA. It's a very reasonable question.

GERTRUDE. No one is questioning your reason.

AGATHA. Just my motive. I don't mean to frighten you, Bernadette, but –

GERTRUDE. Put on some music, Alice.

BERNADETTE. It's all right, Miss Stein. I don't mind.

ALICE. But –

BERNADETTE. France could fall. (*Beat.*) At any minute, couldn't it fall? Miss Stein? (*Beat.*) Miss Toklas?

Beat.

GERTRUDE. Yes.

ALICE. Yes. It could, but –

BERNADETTE. What then?

GERTRUDE. I don't know. I haven't got an answer for that one.

Beat. A silence passes over them.

DOROTHY. I liked Gertrude's idea. Let's put on some music!

AGATHA. I suppose a little music never hurt anyone…

ALICE (*walking to the radio*). We never turn this thing on –

DOROTHY. Put on something fun.

ALICE. Let's see…

DOROTHY. Something we could dance to!

DOROTHY. Glenn Miller!

AGATHA. I'm not quite sure that's how it works, Miss Parker… You can't just press a button and play whatever you like.

DOROTHY. Oh, but if you could! Wouldn't that be something?

ALICE. Which one is it, Bernadette? I can never remember which –

BERNADETTE. Here.

She turns on the radio. It's the middle of a song. Something peppy. Charles Trent, perhaps. DOROTHY *rises.*

DOROTHY. Who will dance with me?

GERTRUDE. I prefer to dance alone.

DOROTHY. Alice –

ALICE. No, no…

DOROTHY. Mary! How about you?

MARY. I don't do much dancing…

DOROTHY. That's very sad, darling.

MARY. I haven't much time these days...

DOROTHY. You've got to *make* time! *Especially* for fun! Come on, Mary... Don't make me stand here by myself, bopping up and down –

LILLIAN (*entering*). Nobody's making you do anything, Dorothy. The only one making you make a fool out of yourself is you.

AGATHA. Well, well, well...

ALICE. Hello, Lillian.

LILLIAN. I could hear the music –

GERTRUDE. Did it disturb your sulking?

LILLIAN. As a matter of fact, it did! Bernadette, a martini, please.

DOROTHY (*at the radio*). How do I... Can we make this louder?

She fumbles with a dial and changes the station. We hear the voice of Philippe Pétain, announcing the surrender of France.

GERTRUDE. Wait!

DOROTHY. But –

GERTRUDE. Leave it on.

LILLIAN. What is it?

GERTRUDE. Shush!

DOROTHY. I don't understand!

GERTRUDE. Dottie, shush!

Beat. They listen quietly. Some understand, some do not.

(*After a moment.*) Turn it off. (*Beat.*) Turn it off, I can't listen to it any longer!

DOROTHY *hesitates.*

Turn it off!

She does. Beat.

ALICE. It can't be.

DOROTHY. Will someone please explain what's happening?

ALICE. I never thought…

LILLIAN. He just surrendered, Dorothy.

ALICE. How could he?

DOROTHY. How could *who*?

LILLIAN. Philippe Pétain! He surrendered.

GERTRUDE. France has fallen.

DOROTHY. Oh, God!

ALICE. I *never* thought.

LILLIAN. I told you he would.

ALICE. We'll have to go back to America! Gertrude, we'll
have to –

GERTRUDE. I don't want to.

LILLIAN. Well, you haven't much choice now, have you?
A traitor to his people!

GERTRUDE. Oh, shut up, Lily!

ALICE. She's right, Gert. We have to go. We've no choice now.

AGATHA. But how will you get out? You're in German
territory now, ladies.

GERTRUDE. We're Americans.

AGATHA. But *she* isn't.

She points at BERNADETTE. *The room grows quiet.*

ALICE. You'll come with us. All right, Bernadette? I promise –
you will come with us.

BERNADETTE. How?

GERTRUDE. It won't happen again.

LILLIAN. What won't?

GERTRUDE. I promised you, Bernadette, and Gertrude Stein never breaks a promise. It will not happen again.

LILLIAN. What is she talking about, Alice?

GERTRUDE. Stay out of it, Lily Ann!

LILLIAN. Are you a Jew? Is she a Jew?

GERTRUDE. It isn't any of your concern!

AGATHA. I'm afraid it is, Gertrude. Everyone in this house is in danger.

GERTRUDE. If we wanted you to know, we would've told you during hors d'oeuvres.

DOROTHY. But you haven't served any!

BERNADETTE. Yes, Miss Hellman. I am a Jew.

AGATHA. Oh, dear.

BERNADETTE. And it's only a matter of time before –

GERTRUDE. It will not happen again!

LILLIAN. What won't? (*Beat.*) What won't happen again, Bernadette?

Beat. BERNADETTE *shrugs and looks at* GERTRUDE.

BERNADETTE. A little curiosity never killed anyone.

DOROTHY. Except for the cat.

ALICE (*to* BERNADETTE). Are you sure?

BERNADETTE. Yes.

Beat.

ALICE. Gertie had an ulcer.

GERTRUDE. A real bastard, that one was.

ALICE. We had been in Germany.

GERTRUDE. Berlin.

ALICE. Gertrude was reading some poetry for an audience.

GERTRUDE. And in the middle of a poem...

ALICE. She sort of...

GERTRUDE. Collapsed.

ALICE. On stage, sort of grabbing her stomach. Like this. (*Demonstrates*.)

GERTRUDE. They understand.

ALICE. They rushed her to the nearest hospital and, you know, we were all obviously very tense not just because she was in pain but because this was only, what –

BERNADETTE. Three years ago.

ALICE. Thank you. And Jews were... being looked at differently. You know?

GERTRUDE. They know.

ALICE. And we're...

AGATHA. Yes.

GERTRUDE. While we were in the waiting room, they brought in a young girl. A little thing.

ALICE. Maybe eighteen.

BERNADETTE. Nineteen.

ALICE. She was covered in blood.

GERTRUDE. Her own.

ALICE. All over... here. (*Waves her hand over her groin*.) And it looked like –

GERTRUDE. It didn't look like, it was!

ALICE. Like it was coming from her Secret Place. All this blood coming from *inside* of her.

AGATHA. I think I've heard enough.

GERTRUDE. You thought wrong. Go on, Alice.

ALICE. Six men had gang-raped her in a bathroom at Lehrter Bahnhof.

GERTRUDE. The train station.

ALICE. One of them had a steel rod.

GERTRUDE. It was a pipe.

ALICE. And he –

GERTRUDE. – inserted –

ALICE. Yes.

GERTRUDE. – into her.

LILLIAN. I don't need to know any more.

BERNADETTE. But you asked.

ALICE. The steel tore through her cervix. I thought she would bleed out, there was so much blood. But it finally stopped, just as Gertie was getting into a bed.

GERTRUDE. I was going to spend the night there.

ALICE. They made me leave. Because I was only a 'friend'. Or because they knew we were Jews.

GERTRUDE. There was a curtain between the girl's bed and mine. I couldn't see much. Just a sliver. A silhouette. I spoke to her through it.

BERNADETTE. You read me poetry.

Beat.

GERTRUDE. I read you poetry. (*Beat.*) Sometimes I thought she was sleeping and sometimes I thought she was dead but one time I thought she was listening. I was released the next day.

ALICE. Gertrude went back every day for hours.

GERTRUDE. Sometimes five.

ALICE. She read her more poetry. Every single day... Until she... Until Bernadette was released.

GERTRUDE. And then we took her home.

DOROTHY. Who were they? The men?

GERTRUDE. Who else?

ALICE. Nazis. Six of them.

BERNADETTE. It wasn't a pipe, though. That part you got wrong. It was a gun, not a pipe. It was cold. And, you know, I had been quiet for a while. I'd left my body. Or I was trapped inside it. But I left, when they were doing their business, I left. But when he came, the last one, the big one, and he put it – inside – me, the gun... I looked at him. Hard. And I begged him to pull the trigger because I wouldn't have to feel it any more. The bullet would have already been inside me. It wouldn't have had to fight its way through skin and bones. *Schießen Sie mich*, I said. *Shoot me!* But he didn't. He didn't shoot even though I begged him to. Maybe because he knew it would be a *freundlichkeit*... A kindness. And there was none of that in his blood. Or maybe because there was some kindness hidden away somewhere and maybe he was sorry. I think about that sometimes. Why. I think about why he didn't shoot.

AGATHA. He was frightened of his power.

GERTRUDE. Power is a frightening thing.

BERNADETTE. I take three or four baths a day, now. I take them only hot. Scalding. And I avoid the mirror completely. Sometimes I wait till there is steam and the water has reached a too-hot point and I step inside. My skin sizzles like an egg on a sidewalk in August. I scrub furiously. A little too furiously. A little too tough on the skin, but it's necessary to get truly clean. To get *sterile*, is how I like to put it. It used to be more. Baths, I mean. Sometimes as many as fourteen. (*Beat.*) But now it's only three. Or four.

MARY. Then there was no café?

ALICE *and* GERTRUDE. No.

MARY. Or any advertisement.

ALICE *and* GERTRUDE. No.

LILLIAN. There was pity.

   Beat.

ALICE *and* GERTRUDE. Yes.

LILLIAN. You'll never have children.

BERNADETTE. These are my children. I take care of them.

GERTRUDE. And we are her mothers.

DOROTHY. When? When did this happen?

BERNADETTE. It has been some time.

LILLIAN. How long?

BERNADETTE. Three years. Maybe more. Maybe less. I don't count the days.

LILLIAN. That's a lie.

DOROTHY. Lillian, don't be cruel.

LILLIAN. But it is! Isn't it, Bernadette? It *is* a lie?

BERNADETTE. Yes.

LILLIAN. You count them all.

BERNADETTE. Every single one.

LILLIAN. You write them down.

BERNADETTE. All of them.

LILLIAN. You mark time.

AGATHA. That's enough, Lillian.

BERNADETTE. I'm marking it now.

LILLIAN. You would've rather died.

DOROTHY. Lillian!

BERNADETTE. I begged him to pull the trigger!

LILLIAN. How many days?

BERNADETTE. One thousand, one hundred and twenty-three days. I was nineteen years old.

AGATHA. Like my Rosalind.

BERNADETTE. Like your Rosalind.

MARY. Did they know you were a Jew?

BERNADETTE. Yes. I think.

DOROTHY. Why were you in Berlin? Wasn't it dangerous for –

BERNADETTE. I was pregnant. There was a doctor…

DOROTHY. Oh, God. You poor girl.

BERNADETTE. Do you think it was my punishment?

AGATHA. For what?

LILLIAN. Punishment for what?

BERNADETTE. Wanting to get rid of it?

AGATHA. Of course not!

ALICE *and* LILLIAN. No!

DOROTHY. But you didn't! You didn't get rid of it, did you?

BERNADETTE. No. The soldiers did it for me.

DOROTHY. Do you know how much it costs? In America? Do any of you know how much it costs to get rid of a baby? Thirty dollars. It costs thirty dollars. You walk into a room; a kitchen, usually. They haven't got hospitals for this sort of a thing. And you give him your thirty dollars and he tells you to lie down on his kitchen table and you hike your skirt up which is how you got in trouble in the first place and the table is very cold so your teeth start to chatter and this man, this doctor says, 'Would you like a glass of water before we begin?' 'I haven't had a glass of water in a dozen years,' I said. 'Have you got any gin?' He did. I drank it. He did the deed. And I went home feeling empty and swollen at the same time. (*Beat.*) It's awful, isn't it?

ALICE (*after a long moment*). I should make those drinks.

BERNADETTE. No. No, I –

ALICE. Sit.

BERNADETTE. Please. Let me make the drinks. It helps me count the days.

Beat.

ALICE. All right...

Beat. BERNADETTE *exits into the kitchen to make the drinks. The silence settles for a moment and then...*

LILLIAN. Bastards.

DOROTHY. Monsters!

AGATHA. It's evil. Whatever moves them, it's evil.

ALICE. It will kill us all, this war.

GERTRUDE. Or the pain of it.

DOROTHY. And they wonder why I drink.

GERTRUDE. Who does?

DOROTHY. People!

GERTRUDE. Everyone drinks these days.

LILLIAN. And if they don't, they're fools.

DOROTHY. The poor little thing...

GERTRUDE. She's tougher than you think, Dottie.

DOROTHY. It's not the tragedies that kill us, y'know... It's the little *messes*... The *little* wars.

Beat.

MARY. What if we could get her out? (*Beat.*) There are calls I could make.

LILLIAN. And how would a psychiatrist from New Jersey *possibly* be of any help in a situation like this?

MARY. We can all help.

LILLIAN. How? Please, Miss Buttinger, do tell me. What can any of us do? Not just for her, but for – For all of them!

MARY. We waste so much time being silent. Do you realise that? Do any of you realise just how much time we waste being silent?

LILLIAN. It's a little too late to raise our voices now. Don't you think?

MARY. As long as people are dying, Miss Hellman, it is never too late. (*Beat.*) Last week, I held my hand over the mouth of a child. A little boy. Because he wanted to scream when he saw them take his mother. My friend. But we'd already decided. If anyone asked, he was mine. My little boy. I'm sorry, officer, I left his papers at home. And if he screamed or cried or got away from me, they'd know. And they'd take him too. (*Beat.*) That's a fact. But it's not so bad. (*Beat.*) Do you know what they do to the children? The ones too little to work? Do you know?

LILLIAN. Enough.

MARY They kill them. And bury them all together. One mass grave for fifty little babies.

AGATHA. I think we have all heard enough, Miss Buttinger.

MARY. Then it's time for me to go. (*Heads for the closet to collect her things*.) Miss Toklas, Miss Stein, thank you, but –

ALICE. But where will you sleep?

She follows MARY *to the closet,* GERTRUDE *rising and standing by her seat.*

MARY. The train station. It will only be a few more hours –

ALICE. But won't that be dangerous?

MARY. Of course, it will. But there's nothing I can do about that now, is there?

AGATHA. There's something you aren't telling us, Miss Buttinger.

GERTRUDE. Please, Monsieur Poirot, give it a rest –

AGATHA. Who are you?

    MARY *ignores her as* BERNADETTE *re-enters with drinks.*

ALICE. You mustn't forget the hat –

MARY. If you need anything –

AGATHA. Come on, now, spit it out –

MARY. If there is anything I can do to help –

GERTRUDE. We know how to find you.

AGATHA. As if a person wouldn't be curious!

    As MARY *is taking the hat from* ALICE, *she loses her grip and the hat falls to the floor. The francs spill out and all eyes are on the pile of smuggled cash.*

LILLIAN. Well!

DOROTHY. Oh!

    MARY *and* ALICE *have rushed to the floor to clean it up as quickly as possible.*

MARY. I'm sorry. I thought – I lost my grip and –

LILLIAN. Look, Aggie, darling! It's like right out of one of your stories.

AGATHA. And you all wondered why I couldn't quench my curiosity.

DOROTHY. Paging Monsieur Poirot!

AGATHA. What's going on, you three?

LILLIAN. Yes, on with it! We haven't got all day!

GERTRUE. Leave it alone, Lily.

LILLIAN. Thousands of francs fall out of a hat and you want me to 'leave it alone'?

GERTRUDE. Precisely.

AGATHA. Let's hear it.

DOROTHY. Yes, dear. And no bullshit.

GERTRUDE. It's none of your business!

LILLIAN. The hell it isn't!

AGATHA. Spit it out, Lady Mary.

MARY. My name isn't Mary.

GERTRUDE. Don't.

MARY. What, then? What would you have me do? I trust them. (*Beat.*) Don't you?

GERTRUDE. Yes. Of course. (*Beat.*) Even Lily Ann. But still. Be careful.

MARY. It's too late for 'careful'. See what happens when I have a little Scotch?

She laughs. DOROTHY *does too.*

My hands shake. And I say so many things I shouldn't.

DOROTHY. Welcome to the table, darling.

LILLIAN. Save it for The Algonquin, Dottie.

AGATHA. Come on then.

LILLIAN. On with it!

MARY/MURIEL. My name isn't Mary. (*Beat.*) It's Muriel.

AGATHA. I walk in the door and intrigue follows me.

MURIEL. I'm Mary when I travel. My real name is Muriel Gardiner. Mary is my code name.

AGATHA. It was obvious.

GERTRUDE. Really, inspector?

MURIEL. My *husband* is Joseph Buttinger. He is the –

AGATHA. The Leader of the Austrian Revolutionary Socialists. We know who he is.

MURIEL. He –

LILLIAN. – is a criminal.

MURIEL. No! He's a hero.

AGATHA. One can*not* be both, my dear. (*A chuckle*.) I suppose that's the *first* lesson of mystery writing.

LILLIAN. In Europe, he's a criminal. And in wartime, Miss Gardiner, your company puts us all at risk.

MURIEL. He is very welcome in Paris.

LILLIAN. Not any more he isn't.

AGATHA. And just how did an American spy wind up in Gertrude Stein's house?

MURIEL. I'm not a spy.

AGATHA. What then?

MURIEL. I'm helping my husband. He has – *We* have been smuggling passports over the border. (*Beat*.) To Jews, mostly. And others, too. I came here because Miss Stein and Miss Toklas were... *are* –

GERTRUDE. We've given her some money for passports.

DOROTHY. But aren't you Americans?

GERTRUDE. They aren't for us, Dotty.

LILLIAN. Christ, Gertie...

GERTRUDE. What?

LILLIAN. You've put yourself in a load of danger.

GERTRUDE. It's Miss Gardiner who is risking everything, Lily Ann. Not I. Not Alice.

MURIEL. If all goes according to plan, I will cross the border tomorrow afternoon with three passports sewn into the lining of my hat. I will be able to rescue three people with what Miss Stein and Miss Toklas have given. Of course, things will be a little more difficult now that France... (*Beat.*) I wasn't supposed to stay. I wasn't supposed to be here, meeting all of you. I was *supposed* to be sleeping in the train station but something... changed...

LILLIAN. Yes. The company.

MURIEL. No. That didn't –

AGATHA. Oh, come now. You weren't curious?

DOROTHY. There is no cure for curiosity.

MURIEL. It wasn't about –

AGATHA. Then what made you stay? Did Gertrude Stein hold up a gun to your head?

GERTRUDE. I?

AGATHA. Who else? Alice?

DOROTHY. Certainly not Alice.

LILLIAN. Every revolutionary wants to meet a famous writer, Miss Gardiner. Of course, you stayed.

DOROTHY. Just how much of this money actually goes to your mission?

MURIEL. Every bit.

DOROTHY. And how much does it cost?

MURIEL. Roughly two hundred francs.

DOROTHY *begins to reach into her pocketbook.*

LILLIAN. There are millions of Jews, Miss Gardiner.

MURIEL. I know.

LILLIAN. What makes you think you can save them all?

MURIEL. I can't.

LILLIAN. Then why save three?

MURIEL. Because an entire race will die.

DOROTHY. And what about Bernadette? Can you help her?

Beat.

MURIEL. If I move quickly, yes. But –

DOROTHY. What? But what?

MURIEL. We'll need more. It won't be easy. Especially now.

DOROTHY *opens her purse and strides over to the hat with money in her hand.*

DOROTHY. I haven't got very much, darling… But it's something.

GERTRUDE. Dorothy –

DOROTHY. Please. Take it.

Beat. MURIEL *takes the money.*

AGATHA. You'll get her out, then? Bernadette?

MURIEL. I will certainly try, Miss Christie.

AGATHA *begins to dig through her purse.*

LILLIAN. And just how much success have you had thus far?

MURIEL. A great deal, Miss Hellman. A great deal.

LILLIAN *begins to search through her purse.*

AGATHA. Here. Take this. (*Hands* MURIEL *the money.*) And yes, Miss Gardiner, I am a 'friend of the Jews'.

MURIEL. Thank you, Miss Christie. (*Beat.*) One never knows.

AGATHA. It isn't a very challenging mystery. I'm an Englishwoman surrounded by Jews in the middle of the Alps. Even Dashiell Hammett could figure that one out. Sorry, Lily.

LILLIAN. What has Dashiell got to do with anything?

ALICE. You can't possibly carry all of this money in that little hat. What if they catch you?

MURIEL. It is worth the risk.

BERNADETTE *re-enters with the drinks. She hands* DOROTHY *hers and leaves* LILLIAN's *on the table.*

LILLIAN. Has anyone got a match?

DOROTHY. What for?

LILLIAN. I'd like to light this cigarette.

DOROTHY. You're not going to –

LILLIAN. What? Not going to what?

DOROTHY. Never mind.

LILLIAN. Don't do that, Dorothy. Don't say 'never mind' because you never actually mean 'never mind'.

GERTRUDE. I believe that Dottie was asking if you'd be donating to Miss Gardiner's cause.

LILLIAN. Why? What can one woman do?

MURIEL. A lot.

LILLIAN. How many have you rescued so far?

MURIEL. Nearly two hundred.

AGATHA. Remarkable!

DOROTHY. Extraordinary.

LILLIAN. But only a fraction of our people.

MURIEL. What do you care how *many* you're saving as long as you're saving some?

LILLIAN. It isn't that I don't care, Miss Gardiner. I never said that I don't care. I simply don't see the point in suicide. (*Beat.*) How many more will you save?

MURIEL. As many as I can.

LILLIAN. But there will always be more Jews.

MURIEL. Not if this continues.

LILLIAN. Don't you think it's all a little in vain, this mission? You and your fraction?

GERTRUDE *rises. Slowly. Then speaks.*

GERTRUDE. What is vain about saving lives?

LILLIAN. It's a fantasy. We can't stop it. And when it's over, because some day it will be over, it will happen again. The Jews will never be normal. They'll never be safe. And some little shrink from the Boons of America will not be our Golem.

GERTRUDE. I have often wondered what it would be like to be normal. I have questioned my sanity and searched for my normalness. I have stood in the yard with my hands clenched in fists yelling into the sky asking why I was not normal. Even though I'm not sure there is a man in the sky. Even though I'm not sure there is a God or a Higher Power or some Holy Spirit… Even though I have questions, so many questions… I have *also* often wondered if normal even exists. I loved you and I hated you when I saw *The Children's Hour*. I had gone to the theatre that night in disguise just in case you were there because conversation with you bores me. But then the curtain went up and there I was in all my ugliness – in all my rage – in all my not-normalness and I realised that I'd been looking at the sky when I should have been looking at myself. (*Beat.*) This is a time that passes. But it takes time – like a stone in your kidney or a rock in your chest – in your heart. But when it passes – when the time passes and you finally realise – it is oh so very normal, oh so very quiet – oh so very yes – yes – *yes*. For me it was a summer afternoon when the sun was hot and melting everything and Alice looked at me. And the sunlight reflected back at me through her eye like a diamond but without the sharpness that can cut your skin like glass. And in her eye I saw yes. I tasted it. I held it in my hands. I kept it safe. In my peripheral vision I can see Alice nodding but I will not look at her because it will make my final point null and void. I want to keep your eyes while I talk to you, Lily Ann. I want to see into your soul. The Jews will never be normal if this madness goes ignored. The yes will never yes. Yes? Yes! I have always known you were a bitch but I've never thought you were a fool. Open your purse. Say yes.

Beat.

LILLIAN. Muriel Gardiner.

MURIEL. Yes?

LILLIAN. I admire what you're doing. I do. I admire your tenacity. I admire your strength. But I worry you feel it is a duty.

MURIEL. It is.

LILLIAN. We can't stop it from happening. We can only slow it.

MURIEL. But something must be done!

LILLIAN. It isn't that I don't like a challenge. I'm Lillian Hellman, darling, of course I like a challenge. I *appreciate* a challenge. I encourage them. And it certainly isn't that I don't care. I'm a Jew, Miss Gardiner, of course I care. But I haven't got a death wish. And I certainly don't want to wind up writing my next play in a labour camp.

AGATHA. How would you write if you haven't got any paper?

LILLIAN. Writers always find a way.

MURIEL. And so do psychiatrists, Miss Hellman. Or anyone, really. It's called surviving.

GERTRUDE. And surviving is an art.

AGATHA. *Are* you even a psychiatrist? Forgive me for wondering, dear, but I suppose that's Lesson Number Two!

MURIEL. Yes. Yes, Miss Christie, I really *am* a psychiatrist. Though I've almost forgotten what it's like. I'm turning into someone else. Into Mary. I'm turning more and more into her every day.

LILLIAN. It happens. I used to be 'honest'. I used to be 'brave', too. And, Miss Gardiner, I was 'responsible'. Someone called me 'powerful' and 'assertive' and another said I was 'intelligent'. And… then one day I was something else.

GERTRUDE. A bitch.

LILLIAN. Yes… That.

GERTRUDE. When did it happen?

LILLIAN. Overnight, I think. One day I wasn't, and one day I was. But you see, a person can only hear 'no' so many times. 'But you're a woman', 'but the characters are women', 'what if you make it a man'. A woman can only hear that so many times before she goes mad. And maybe I throw an ashtray or seven and use the occasional 'fuck' in passing and maybe I do smoke two packs of Camels a day just so I can blow it in their faces. (*Beat*.) But I do what I've got to do when I want to make a point. When I want to get my way. (*Beat. A revelation*.) That's why you stayed. Isn't it, Miss Gardiner? To make a point?

MURIEL. I don't –

LILLIAN. With *us*… With us you might even get your way!

MURIEL. No.

LILLIAN. Did you come here expecting an army, Miss Gardiner? A legion of writers? Did you think we would all go home, call the papers, our publishers, expose everything? Did you think we would put targets on our backs?

MURIEL. I had no idea that you were coming.

LILLIAN. I don't believe that.

ALICE. We weren't expecting Miss Gardiner until tomorrow, Lillian.

LILLIAN. It's neurotic to think about the things we cannot change, Miss Gardiner. It's psychotic dwelling on them!

MURIEL. I'm not dwelling, I'm doing!

LILLIAN. And what happens if you get caught?

MURIEL. Someone else will take over.

LILLIAN. Are you sure?

MURIEL. I can hope.

LILLIAN. And that's how you sleep at night? With hope?

Beat.

MURIEL. I am certain, Miss Hellman, that when I sleep, I sleep far better than you ever have and ever will.

A long beat. Uncomfortably long. This is when we learn that LILLIAN *is vulnerable, too. After a moment, she reaches into her purse and digs around.*

LILLIAN. Three hundred francs.

MURIEL. Thank you.

LILLIAN. I must ask these questions, you know.

MURIEL. I don't. But thank you.

LILLIAN. Writers are curious people, Miss Gardiner.

GERTRUDE. And cruel, too. (*Beat.*) That isn't an insult, Lily, it's a fact.

LILLIAN. And you'll help her? The girl?

GERTRUDE. Her name is Bernadette.

Beat. For the first time, BERNADETTE *realises what is happening.*

MURIEL. We'll get her a passport. If she travels with an American… with *me* –

BERNADETTE. But I can't leave them –

GERTRUDE. Nonsense.

MURIEL. We'll have to be quick, Bernadette. It's going to become very dangerous very quickly in France.

BERNADETTE. But this is my home –

ALICE. You'll find another.

MURIEL. And you mustn't speak, not to anyone. If they ask you questions, I'll answer. They ask less questions if you're with an American. If they insist, keep your answers short. You'll have to – Miss Stein, she'll have to come with me now…

GERTRUDE. Go. Go and pack your things.

BERNADETTE. But –

GERTRUDE. The clock is ticking and it never stops for anyone.

BERNADETTE. Miss Toklas –

Beat.

ALICE. Go on, dear.

MURIEL. Don't pack too much! Only what you can carry.

Beat. BERNADETTE *nods and exits. A moment passes.*

ALICE. The house will feel so empty.

AGATHA. Won't you go too?

ALICE. Only when we absolutely have to.

GERTRUDE. France is our home.

ALICE. For now…

GERTRUDE. Yes. For now…

LILLIAN (*to* MURIEL). You'll hide it in your hat, then? The money?

MURIEL. Yes.

LILLIAN. That's a lot of money for a little hat.

MURIEL. Well…

LILLIAN. Why Mary?

MURIEL. It was assigned to me.

LILLIAN. Mary was the Virgin Mother of Jesus Christ.

MURIEL. I know that.

LILLIAN. A Catholic Saint Rescuing the Jews? Sounds like an assignment from the Vatican.

MURIEL. It was picked at random.

LILLIAN. May I see the hat?

MURIEL. Here. (*Hands it to her.*)

LILLIAN. Are there others? Couriers, I mean?

MURIEL. Yes.

LILLIAN. Do we know them?

MURIEL. You might.

LILLIAN. Are they powerful?

MURIEL. Some.

LILLIAN. Writers?

MURIEL. I know of one.

LILLIAN. Actors?

MURIEL. Several.

DOROTHY. Socialites?

MURIEL. Many.

AGATHA. What about Englishwomen?

MURIEL. And a few men, too.

LILLIAN. And psychiatrists.

Beat.

MURIEL. Just one.

LILLIAN. What happens if they ask to inspect your hat?

MURIEL. I wrap it in silk. It masks the change in texture.

LILLIAN. And there are writers, you say?

MURIEL. One.

LILLIAN. Who? Tell me who.

MURIEL. I can't put them at risk. But *she* has saved many.

LILLIAN. How many?

MURIEL. One hundred, at least.

Beat.

LILLIAN. Alice.

ALICE. Mmm?

LILLIAN. Get me my hat.

Beat. No one moves.

Quickly, now. Get me my hat.

ALICE *rushes to get the hat.*

MURIEL. Miss Hellman?

LILLIAN. Why Germany?

MURIEL. There is a family there who needs our help. And then I will return to Austria.

LILLIAN. Why not do both at the same time?

MURIEL. How do you suggest – ?

LILLIAN. I'll take it to Germany. (*Takes her hat from* ALICE.) Thank you. And scissors, dear. A little needle and thread, too.

DOROTHY. You can't be serious.

LILLIAN. I most certainly can.

AGATHA. You're not thinking straight, Lillian.

LILLIAN. How hard can it be?

MURIEL. Your heart pounds constantly. You're always afraid there is someone behind you. Someone who knows. Someone who might kill you. Or arrest you. Arrest would be worse. If

they arrest you, they'll torture you. My friend, Misha... he
was caught some weeks ago. They found the passports sewn
into the lining of his coat. We promised each other we'd keep
going. If one of us was caught, we'd keep going. No looking
back. Because if you look back, you miss the train. Or the
boat. If you look back, you're next. So I kept going. Even
when his wife called to say they'd found him, cold as ice, lips
blue as the sky, with a body so mangled and tortured she
barely recognised him. Even then I kept going. Because there
was a train. Or a boat. And a schedule. Some days I'd go
without eating. Or sleeping. Or both! You have to make
sacrifices if you want to succeed. (*Beat.*) It's like this, Miss
Hellman: You can't duck inside when it starts raining because
you're on a schedule and soon your boots are soaked
completely through and even when you think you might
drown inside those boots you have to keep walking because
everything you do is on a schedule. A very tight schedule.
And you must stick to it, because if you veer even the littlest
bit off-course, you might endanger the entire mission.

LILLIAN. I've been wearing hats for years, darling. Unless
these francs are seven thousand pounds, I think I'll be just
fine.

Beat. Another beat. And another. After a moment,
GERTRUDE *starts to laugh. She is joined by* ALICE, *then*
AGATHA, *then* DOROTHY *and finally... finally,* MURIEL.

GERTRUDE. Oh, Lily...

LILLIAN. What?

DOROTHY. She'll never change...

MURIEL. What would we call you? You'd need a code name.

LILLIAN. Who gets to decide that?

MURIEL. No one in particular.

DOROTHY. How about Helen?

LILLIAN. Boring!

AGATHA. Mildred.

LILLIAN. Too stuffy!

MURIEL. Edna?

LILLIAN. Edna Ferber is a hack!

ALICE. Katherine!

LILLIAN. Too simple!

GERTRUDE. I think I've got it.

LILLIAN. Go on.

> *As* GERTRUDE *speaks,* BERNADETTE *re-enters. She has changed into street clothes and carries a small suitcase. No one notices as they listen to* GERTRUDE. BERNADETTE *moves to the coat-rack –* MURIEL *has still not removed hers – and prepares to leave.*

GERTRUDE. There is a river in Switzerland. Just over the mountains in the Albula Range. Its water is a crystalline blue. The Romans used the road for many years. In fact, there is a ruin of an Ancient Roman temple there. Without the river, the Romans wouldn't have been able to sustain themselves. A hat with money and silk in its lining seems to me to have a lot in common with that river.

LILLIAN. What's it called?

GERTRUDE. Julia.

> LILLIAN *blows a raspberry as the lights dim around* BERNADETTE. *She places her suitcase on the ground and begins to speak.*

BERNADETTE. The women never went to sleep that night, except for Agatha Christie, who had been the first to leave. She was tired. Or bored. She refused to confess which. She developed Alzheimer's disease in her later years, so who knows what memories of this night stayed? Dorothy Parker returned to London, where she would spend another month before returning to America. After a long battle with alcoholism, she died of a massive heart attack at the age of seventy-three. (*Beat.*) Alice B. Toklas outlived Gertrude

Stein by twenty-*one* years. She would publish a memoir
titled *What is Remembered* in 1963. It left little doubt that
Gertrude Stein was the love of her life. She died alone and in
poverty, no longer surrounded by the luxuries of art. (*Beat*.)
Muriel Gardiner would rescue hundreds more before the
war's end. And me. Bernadette Marienthal. I would never
have children. At least, none of my own. The soldiers
thought they'd silenced me, but instead, they made a teacher
of me. There would be twenty students a year. For thirty-two
years! Six hundred and forty minds discovering my friends.
And with each passing season, we'd dissect a poem of
Gertrude's. 'I knew her,' I'd say. 'And I knew her friends.'
Before the war. And after. 'They rescued me,' I told my
stupefied students. 'In so very many ways.' (*Beat*.) We got
on separate trains that morning; Miss Hellmann headed to
Germany. Miss Gardiner and I travelled a much longer
distance. What she did in Germany, what sights her hat may
have seen, what stories she would tell would remain a
mystery to us for many years to come. Miss Gardiner
returned to her practice and spent the rest of her years in
Princeton, New Jersey. It was there that she would read
Lillian Hellman's 1973 memoir *Pentimento*, which featured
a chapter about a young woman who rescued Jews during the
Second World War. A young woman who seemed so very
familiar. With all of the witnesses gone, it wouldn't surprise
a soul that Lillian would borrow a little inspiration from
Gertrude and name the mysterious woman after a river in
Switzerland. Well, not all of the witnesses... I would survive
them all. (*Beat*.) Though she'd never confess, not even on
her deathbed in 1984, Lillian had known the real Julia: the
Little Psychiatrist from Princeton. 'Tell us about them all,
Miss Marienthal!' they'd beg me, my surrogate children. 'I'll
tell you when I'm dead,' I'd say. 'I'll tell you when I'm dead
and buried.'

Blackout.

End of play.

www.nickhernbooks.co.uk

facebook.com/nickhernbooks

twitter.com/nickhernbooks